SHIVA SUTRAS

शिव सुत्र

Gurudev Sri Sri Ravi Shankar

Sri Sri Publications Trust, India

Shiva Sutras

1st Edition September 2010

Published by:

THE ART OF LIVING

Sri Sri Publications Trust
Art of Living International Centre,
21st KM, Kanakapura Road, Udaypura, Bangalore - 560082
Email: info@srisripublications.com
Website: www.sattvastore.com
Toll Free 1800-258-8888

ISBN: 9789380592800

Layout by: Sri Sri Publications Trust

Printed in India by: Pentaplus Printers Pvt Ltd., Bengaluru-560044

Contents

PREFACE

In this edition, below the sutras is a paraphrase of each sutra in English. This addition will be useful for readers wishing to review the sutras and their meaning without having to re-read the whole book. True to the meaning of a sutra, the translations capture the essence of each sutra in few words full of meaning. The paraphrase in most cases has been taken directly from Gurudev's commentary, and where necessary, slightly edited for conciseness.

Sanskrit words have been written in italics and spelt in a regular fashion. This will help those who may be unfamiliar with the sutras but still wish to read them with correct pronunciation. An appendix explaining the spelling and pronunciation is located at the back. Proper names have been made an exception to this system, and have been written according to common conventions.

It is our great pleasure to present to the English-speaking public a translation of Gurudev's Kannada talks on the *Shiva* Sutras. We hope it faithfully delivers the timeless, yet ever new message of the original commentary by Gurudev Sri Sri Ravi Shankar to all seekers on the path.

Jai Gurudev

THE MIND FACING INWARDS IS ALWAYS HAPPY

yasya niścasita vedā yo vedebhyo akhila jagat
nirmama tamaha vande vidyātirtha maheśvara

In order to fly a kite and guide it from the ground, we need a thin thread. While this thread stays on the ground, the kite soars in the air. That thread is a *sutra*. Likewise, for our life to soar higher and expand into the vastness of infinity, what is needed? We need a *sutra* that acts as a link between earth and sky, between humanity and Divinity.

Panini describes a *sutra* as:
Alpāk aramasa digdha sāravat viśvato mukha
Astobhamanavadya ca sūtra sūtravido vidu

"*Alpāk ara asa digdha sāravat viśvato mukha*" – A *sutra* is described as that which contains the essence and expresses the full meaning in a few words. The nature of the *sutra* we hold on to decides the direction and the quality of our life. In everyone's life there is some spark of goodness or auspiciousness. We should reflect whether we are holding on to the good and positive or misfortune and negativity. Regardless of which part we tend to focus on, if we search we can definitely find happiness, pleasure and fortune in some measure. Yet, if you look now, this is not the case. Actually, there is so much that is positive. Life is made up of eighty percent positivity and only twenty percent negativity, the part that causes problems. Yet we make this twenty percent into two thousand percent; usually, we cling to the negative.

In every life some good must have happened, but the nature of mind is that it ignores everything positive and clings only to the negative. Suppose someone approaches you and gives you ten compliments and one insult. What will you remember? The mind's nature is to cling to the negative. In order to change this mindset, we should hold on to the *Shiva Sutras.*

We should hold on to truth, beauty and *śivatattva,* auspiciousness or innocence, wherever they appear in our life. That is the reason for listening to the *Shiva Sutras.* If life does not have a *sutra* to guide it, it is not possible to find happiness, and the kite will fall to the ground. A kite may have everything, including a tail, but without a thread, how can it take off? The *Shiva Sutras* run through everybody's life. That is why it is said:

Namah śrī śambhave svātmānanda prakāśa vapuśe

I bow down to the wealth that brings peace and fills the body with joy.

How does auspiciousness begin? It happens when the mind turns inwards. When the mind goes more and more outside, it gets caught up in problems and confusion. Do you know what misery is? Misery comes when the mind gets caught up in the world and forgets itself. Happiness can be described as remembering yourself.

Suppose a close relative or friend visits after a long time. You prepare sweets, arrange everything nicely to welcome them and go to the railway station with a bouquet of flowers to greet them. You eagerly look for them, checking whether or not the train is running on time and whether they have arrived. How do you feel when you finally meet them? Thrilled! The mind instantly blossoms. Where there is no eagerness and anticipation, there is less love.

The mind naturally flows towards that which you love. When you are with a dear friend, your mind stays with you and does not wander elsewhere. Observe that when you are joyful, you become one with your self. Your nature is joy, and this is the reason you experience joy.

If you read the word "*mana*," meaning mind, in reverse, it becomes "*nama*." When people visit various temples and pray, they say, "*Namah*." What does it mean? When the mind turns inward it is *namah*, but when the mind goes outward, it is *manah*.

What attracts the mind outward? It is prosperity, wealth, success and beauty. The sight of anything beautiful draws the mind towards it. Whether money or fame, the mind gravitates towards it. The whole world revolves around only one thing, and that is "*śrī*," or prosperity. Yearn for knowledge, yearn for happiness, yearn for beauty, wealth, success, advancement – whatever you long for, it is only for one desire, and that is *śrī*. However, the more intensely people long for it, the more difficult it is to attain. That is why everybody wears such long faces, as if everything were shrouded in misery. This is why Buddha concisely said, "Desire is the root cause of misery." Go anywhere and look at what the people talk about, and you will find that it is all about *śrī*. Go to any chamber of commerce or film industry meeting, and what do they discuss, but ways to become rich and famous. That is *śrī*. Or go to any legislative body, and they talk about political power. Even that is *śrī*.

The whole world revolves around *śrī*, but how do we acquire it? Even if we do get it, it will turn out not to be satisfying. If one is to find *śrī*, one's mind must turn inwards. When we are in a state of *namah*, when we are introspective, we find *śrī* and true wealth is born. Real wealth is within us, and when we turn inwards, we can access real happiness and pleasure. Although the richest of the rich may smile outwardly, peep into their minds, and you will not find any cheerfulness or contentment. Without satisfaction, what is the use of such a life and such wealth? It is nothing but worry, worry, and to die with worries. What kind of *śrī* is that?

Sometimes, people do gain wealth and fame, but even that is followed by problems. Once, when one of our ex-prime ministers met me, he confessed, "Before, in summer I used to sleep outside the house on a cot. Now, you can see fifty people around me and security all over. Now I am a prisoner, more so than the actual prisoners in Tihar Jail."

"*Śhambhave*" – Wealth and prosperity should bring peace. However, many times one acquires wealth and many problems follow it. Quarrels start between parents and children and between husband and wife. If you examine the pending court cases, you will find that 75 to 80 percent of the cases arise out of disputes over money! Most of the conflicts between people happen over money, is it not? Even if we were to gain so much wealth, what is the point? While we do need money, along with wealth we also get diseases like stomach pains, ulcers, diabetes, heart attack, etc.

Once, a man won ten lakhs in a lottery. His wife worried how she should break the news to her husband because it might give him a shock or he might even suffer a heart attack due to sheer excitement. So she went to a priest. He said, "Don't worry. I will come with you, and together we'll give him the news." So the next Sunday, he went to their house and asked him, "My child, suppose by the grace of God you were to win ten lakh, what would you do with it?" The man answered, "I'd give half of it to the church, Father." No sooner the priest heard this, he had a heart attack.

Wealth should bring peace. Being wealthy should not bring arrogance, hostility, jealousy, disgust or boredom. Many times, when you receive a gift from someone, your state of mind changes as soon as you receive it. Have you observed this? When you receive certain things, you receive not only the gift but the intention along with the gift. That is the reason why, in the past, people accepted things from others only after careful observation. If they did accept, then they would immediately give a gift in return. An old saying says, "Why should we take others' things that we do not want?" It is because such wealth might bring peace or disturbance. Nobody wants a disturbed mind.

Today we have completely forgotten this tradition. However, there is one thing we did in the past and continue to do today: when we celebrate weddings, religious ceremonies and other rituals, whether on happy or sad occasions, we invite guests for food and after food give them each one rupee as *dakśina*, or offering. This practice is more prevalent in villages. Do you know the reason behind this? This is to express gratitude to the guests for attending the ceremony and eating the food. The belief is that the guests have given them peace, and in this way, certain negative karma leaves and positive karma is restored.

"Śrī śambhave" – wealth should be peaceful. *"Svātmānanda"* – filled with bliss, having a cheerful state of mind. There are some people who do very good acts, but do not have peace and joy. Instead, they are very serious and have long faces. If the world is serious, it cannot be enjoyable, it will be dry and dull. Look at children. They are not very serious. They are happy. What kind of happiness do they have? *"svātmānanda prakāśā vapuse"* – happiness overflows from their bodies. They send out vibrations full of joy.

In life, happiness is the only attraction. You may have noticed that some people who are beautiful and have nice, fair skin are not attractive, while others who are not so pleasant to look at are still attractive. This is because of the vibrations they spread around them – *"Svātmānanda prakāśā."* Wherever a child comes from, whether from China, Africa or North America, it is attractive. Joy overflows from each and every cell of its body. A child's mind is innocent and calm, with a blossomed awareness. This is life's goal. One characteristic of life is that it should end where it began, and life is a cycle that starts with happiness.

"Ānandena jātāni jīvanti" – this is a quotation from the Upanishads: "Life happens in joy and finds completion in joy." The soul should be filled with happiness – that is the goal of the *Shiva Sūtras*: *svātmānanda prakāśa vapuśe.*

That happiness is not limited to us, but spreads to all who come near us. Such happiness is the sign of real success. Some people who do *sadhana*, though they sit from morning till evening with their fingers on their nose doing *pranayama*, shout at anyone who comes close and disturbs them, even children. It means that there has been no reduction in anger. What are you doing? *Sadhana*? Is this a sign of *sadhana*? If this is what *sadhana* means, then it's better to stay away from it.

Many youth have left *sadhana* because of this. In their homes they see their older siblings, parents, grandparents and relatives praying and applying *chandan* to their forehead and to others too. Yet their anger has not lessened, even a bit. Seeing this, young people lose faith. They say, "If this is religious life, we don't need it." It is natural. Many *swamis* who are in charge of *mathas* are like this. They show such uncontrollable anger! People come with devotion, but are revolted by the way they see some *swamis* treating people. They think, "How arrogant!" and become angry and afraid. There is a saying that people should have fear and devotion. This is not correct. Where there is fear, it is impossible to have devotion, and with devotion, fear cannot exist. Both cannot be together. Someone must have compiled that saying sarcastically, but the sarcasm in it has not been properly understood. Instead, people worry that a *swami* will curse them. Devotion vanishes, and only fear is left.

"*Vapuse*" – the body should radiate happiness. Life is complete when that happens. Then, we realise that the aim of life has been reached. "*Svātmānanda prakāśa vapuśe*." This is the goal of the *Shiva Sūtras*. We should read the *sutras* so that this happens. What can we do if this does not happen?

Atha śhiva sūtrah

Then hold on to the *Shiva Sūtras*

After we are asked to hold on to the *Shiva Sūtras*, they are explained one by one. Each *sutra* is complete in itself.

चैतन्यमात्मा
Chaitanyamātmā

We can realise our self to the extent that we raise our energy.

The first *sutra* is "*Chaitanyamātmā.*" You are alive, but you are living as though you were dead. Sleeping, eating and talking - you are like one who walks in his sleep. Often, mothers feed milk to their half-sleeping children, who do not remember anything later. In the morning, they complain that she did not feed them food or milk. We also live like this, as though we eat while we are asleep and continue to slumber. We do not have knowledge of ourself. How do we get knowledge about ourselves and about the soul? Knowledge grows as our energy rises – "*Chaitanyamātmā.*" This is the first *sutra*.

If we succeed in this *sutra*, then we become "*Namah śhrī śambhave svātmānanda prakāśa vapuśe*" – we reach our goal. "*Chaitanyamātmā*" – raise the energy in the body and in life.

The moment our energy is low, our speech gets confused, and we become lazy. When you talk too much, your energy lowers, and you get bored. If you have not experienced this, then do an experiment. Try to abuse someone for one and a half hours continuously, which may or may not even be possible – in a short time your stomach will feel sick.

We lose energy, which is required to digest food, and so the brain also stops working and starts functioning like a fool. Even if we eat more, vitality lowers. Have you experienced this? We are not at our best on a day when we overeat, isn't it?

There are Brahmins who specialise in eating at death ceremonies, especially in Mathura and other such places. They are called "*panda*". Their only job is to eat wherever there is death ceremony. When many people die, they are in great demand and sometimes have to eat at as many as five or six places in a single day!

Once, a son accompanied his father to the ceremony and they had a competition to see who could eat more. During the meal, the son drank a glass of water. The father got angry and slapped his son, asking him, "Why are you drinking instead of eating?" But they were not able to talk about it then. On reaching home, again the father asked the son the same thing. "I drank to settle the food I had eaten so I could eat more." The father slapped him again and said, "Why didn't you tell me there? I could have done the same and eaten more."

On another occasion two ladies, who were neighbors, were talking. One was making the bed for her husband at one in the afternoon and so the other lady asked her, "Why are you making the bed so early?" The first one replied, "My husband has gone for food at a death ceremony. He will have to sleep as soon as he returns home." Hearing that, the other lady said, "That is better. For my husband, I have to send the bed to wherever he has gone for the ceremony. After eating he cannot even make it back home." Eating is also tiring.

Where is your energy if you overeat? It is the same with those who oversleep – they cannot be full of vitality. That is why it is said, "*chaitanyamātmā*." We can realise our self to the extent that we raise our consciousness, our vitality. That is why we should do *pranayama*, *Sudarshan Kriya* and meditation. When you start doing these practices, then consciousness dawns. That is what the first *sutra* means.

You are searching for your self. Your self is not something that is separate from you. Your consciousness is your self, from which everything has been created. It is possible to experience this only when you become one with your consciousness. The same consciousness also makes it possible for you to understand yourself. Only this consciousness can understand itself. As consciousness, or energy, increases knowledge also grows. One who is awake has tremendous consciousness. Even the sleeping man has consciousness; but only the one who is awake knows it while the other one is unaware of it.

"*Chaitanyamātmā*" – this is the first *sutra*. When we look at nature, consciousness is visible in every atom. Only in some it rests in a dormant state, in some it is partially expressed and in others it is expressed in abundance. If one understands this and wakes up to this consciousness, one can reach the ultimate goal. "*Svātmānanda prakāśa vapuśe*" – the light of joy in our body is our consciousness. We chant, do *yagyas* and practice *yoga* in order to raise our level of consciousness and move towards the goal of self-realisation. In fact, raising the level of consciousness is not the right phrase, because consciousness does not increase or decrease. It is only when we realise that everything is consciousness that we start to experience consciousness.

ज्ञानं बन्ध
jñānam bandhah

Limited knowledge creates bondage.

The second *sutra* says, "*jñānam bandhah.*" When we sleep we do not experience bondage. Only after we wake up do we feel bound. What binds us? The experience of 'knowing' creates bondage. Once, a person who was returning from a pilgrimage received the news that his house had caught fire. He was suddenly overwhelmed with fear, agitation and distress and was so shocked that his heart almost stopped. He was caught in bondage even before reaching his house because of the knowledge that he heard. Limited knowledge creates bondage. After some time, another person approached and told him that it was not his house but a neighbor's house that had caught fire. "Is that so? I'm saved!" At once he returned to his normal self. The feeling of "my house" and "mine" created the bondage. That is why the *sutra* says, "*jñānam bandhah*" – knowledge creates bondage. Without obtaining knowledge of the self, of "Who am I?" We go about acquiring knowledge of the world, of "What is this?" and this causes bondage.

Where there is knowledge, the mind is limited. Some awareness is needed. For example, when you drive somewhere you need to have directions. Work requires knowledge, concentration and awareness and when you focus, your mind becomes limited. The real nature of your mind is infinite. However, when we work, the mind becomes limited and limited knowledge binds us. Many people are unable to sleep because they go on thinking. This thinking comes from knowledge. Can you think without having some knowledge?

Good knowledge generates love and affection, while negative knowledge generates anger and hatred. When we see a beautiful object, whether it is nature or a person, there is a desire to possess it and craving starts. Knowledge has created bondage. Similarly, when you see something that is ugly, the mind gets disgusted – knowledge creates bondage. That is why it is said, "*jñānam bandhah*"

Every second in life is new, but the limited knowledge you receive through your five sense-organs at every moment ties you to the past. Every cell in nature is able to perceive, understand and learn. This capacity is consciousness, which is the sign of life. So what is the difference between a wooden peg and a butterfly? At someone's approach a butterfly, sensing danger, will fly off, while a wooden peg will not move. The same consciousness is present in the wooden peg, but to a far lower extent, so much so that some might say it is not present at all.

Even a stone has life, though it is so inert that it appears not to have life. Plants and trees also have emotions, but they are rarely seen. If one takes an axe to a tree, it cries in fear and if one waters a tree, it is happy. However, a tree does not have as much consciousness as birds and animals have to express its emotions. When you show a stick to a dog, it runs away, but when shown a piece of bread, it wags its tail and comes closer. The same feelings are there in trees, but animals can express them more clearly. Although the consciousness in stones is far less, say one percent, it is still there.

It is said that only knowledge will turn a man into a stone. A know-it-all cannot learn anything. There is no life, no vitality in one who is unwilling to learn. Newness is the sign of life. Learning happens only when you feel something is new. The unknown makes you attentive. An expert cyclist can easily become careless, while a beginner will ride with full attention, keeping an eye out for every possible obstacle in the road. To be full of life requires attentiveness and a willingness to learn.

When asked if he knows God, a wise person will simply smile and keep quiet because God is not an object of knowledge. God is knowledge itself as well as the ability to know. God is life, not a thing to acquire. When you say, "I know," your ability to learn becomes less and the vast range of knowledge in front of you is limited. That is why it is said, "*satyam jñānam anantah brahman*" – *Brahma* means truth and infinite knowledge. In order to be free of the bondage of knowledge, the next *sutra* says:

योनिवर्गः कलाशरीरम्
yonivargah kalāśarīram

All activities happen through the body, which itself is an art. The body has originated from and is composed of the five elements.

It is only through the five sense organs that we receive knowledge. "*Yonivargah kalāśarīram*" means that these five sense organs, along with the mind, are all a part of the greater universe.

When you understand this, a witness attitude can arise in you. You can observe: "I am not the mind, the emotions or the sense organs."

We apply ash to the body as a symbol showing that there is no difference between the skin and ash. When one realises that it is only a matter of days before this body turns into ash, it becomes impossible to commit a crime, to kill someone or to break into a house. We call this ash *vibhuti* – "*bhuti*" means experience and "*vibhuti*" means a distinct, special experience. This experience is knowing that though this body will become ashes, "I am the self. My nature is *Shiva*." When this is our real nature, then why should we get angry or jealous over small issues that have no meaning? Ash is applied every day to remind us of this truth again and again.

"*Yonivargah kalāśarīram*" – this body does not belong to us. It is created out of the five elements and belongs to the universe. The banana that was in the market yesterday entered your body this morning and is now ready to hear this talk. Everything that you have eaten, bread, butter, jam, eggplants and potatoes, all of it has been converted into your mind and body and is here, listening to this talk. Reflect on this knowledge and you might be amazed. The type of food you take determines how you think. This is all "*Yonivargah*"

The whole world is one *yoni,* one body. Within that, our body is a work of art. Remember this. Wake up! Look around you and realise that all the different types of bodies have emerged from one consciousness, and your body is also part of this creation. When we were born, we only weighed three to four kilos, but now look at how much we weigh. The 70 to 80 kilos you have gained comes from the earth, water, grains and air, and all of these, including your body, will remain here.

While you are still alive, become one with your body. That is meditation. This may sound surprising. You are not lazy or an inert piece of nature, so you should use your consciousness. However, the *sutra* says just the opposite, "Unite with your body." This is a true statement, and it holds a valuable lesson if we look into it deeply. Before a kite is thrown to fly, it is held back. Similarly, we can understand that we are different from the body, mind and intellect only when we observe them and become one with them. This is the reason why we bring all our attention to each part of the body during *yoga nidra*.

This body is an expression of nature. "*Kalāśarīram*" – this body is a piece of art made up of five elements. One unit of consciousness becomes eye, nose, hands, teeth, tongue and different organs. The ability to see, hear, taste and feel all manifests in the body. What art is greater than this? The whole universe is an art. Nature and anything else that you admire and praise is a piece of art. A dull person does not honour anything, but those with elevated consciousness respect life, honouring everything and everyone. A stone cannot honour nor even love anyone. If you are to admire anything, you need consciousness. You honour all creatures and everyone because you all belong to the same family – "*Yonivargah kalāśarīram*"

If you have learnt to honour others to such a degree, you can be liberated from the bondage of knowledge. In the *Bhagavad Gītā*, *Krishna* says, "*Na hi jñānena sadraśah pavitrah iha vidyate*" –

"only knowledge can purify you." There is no soap like knowledge. However, the arrogance that comes from thinking that you know many things is like the dirt that forms when soap is not properly rinsed out of the clothes after washing. You may have washed the clothes, but you did not rinse out the soap! You cannot wear such clothes – they will begin to smell. The bad smell that comes from intellectual arrogance is worse than the smell that comes from ignorance.

After we escape the bonds of knowledge we feel that everything belongs to us, we are in everyone, and that nothing is different from us. You start to experience such oneness - that my self is the same as anyone else's. "*Sarva bhūtātma bhūtātmah*" – the person that considers that everyone's self is the same as his self has reached truth, consciousness and his goal. Then "*svātmānanda prakāśa vapuśe.*"

When you reach that goal, the happiness that wells up inside is not limited only to you, but radiates like light. If light can be bound, then it is not light. Light's nature is to spread. The twinkling of the stars that is visible today may have shone as many as 1000 years ago! Likewise, it is not happiness if it does not spread. The happiness of a child, who is playing and laughing, is not limited only to that child, but spreads to anyone who comes near. Even an unhappy person looking at a child at play will forget his pain. The goal of life should be to radiate happiness from each and every cell of your being, and that happiness should continue spreading outward. Then knowledge is complete. Otherwise, incomplete knowledge will bind you.

THE ENERGY CENTRES

ज्ञानाधिष्ठानं मातृका

"Jñānādhisthānam mātrka"

Go to the root of knowledge, silence.

"Jñānādhisthānam mātrka" – carefully observe and distinguish the different ideas, thoughts or worries that arise in your mind. Then observe one thought, then one sentence and then one word. Then separate that one word into letters and look at each letter carefully. When you do this, your worries will disappear. Practice this for one week and you will understand that when we hold onto the silence that is in between words, then worries vanish. Where there is no sound or words, there are no worries because words are the root cause of worry. To transcend them is to reach silence. The *sutra* says, *"Jñānādhisthānam mātrka"* – move from knowledge to the highest knowledge. A *mantra*, a sacred sound, is defined as "*manahtrāyate iti mantrah*" – a *mantra* is that which, when repeated constantly, clears your mind from worries and protects you.

Knowledge is bondage, and it is impossible to gain knowledge without words. We need the help of language to understand what we are worrying or not worrying about. When we separate the words, we will be free from worry. One gets worried by holding onto sentences. Suppose your mind is worried that "My son is unemployed." Now sit down and break up each of the words in the sentence, like this: M-y s-o-n i-s u-n-e-m-p-l-o-y-e-d. The intensity of the worry becomes less, and if you reduce its intensity, then the mind, which is entangled in a sentence, drops the worry and becomes contemplative. If you meditate and attempt to drive away the worry, it may not work. So take hold of the worry and go for its root by taking apart its words and meaning.

उद्यमो भैरवः

udyamao bhairavah

When you put in full effort then you experience completeness.

"*Udyamo*" means effort. Give your 100 percent in action, speech and thought, and the energy that is generated by the union of these three will raise you up to a higher level. *Udyamo* is what supports us.

In life, we do so little. We do not give our full effort anywhere and even worry half-heartedly, here and there. If you want to worry, then sit down and worry 100 percent. Are you worried that you may drown or fall sick? You may die, and that is all. If you die, then there will be nothing to worry about. Anyway, everyone has to die.

What is worry? Worry means not applying your efforts 100 percent. You may be worrying about today, tomorrow or even the coming decade. If you are going to worry, then worry big! Worry about how the world will be after 100 or 5000 years. There is so much pollution already in the world today. What will happen after another 15 or 20 years? If you are going to worry, then do it in a big way. Drown yourself in worry. Otherwise, we live as though we are dead or dying at every moment. In Hindi, it is said, "A dying person dies only once, whereas a person afraid of death dies every moment."

When will "*svātmānanda prakāśa vapuśe*" dawn in life? When will life be full of joy? We bargain for a little of this and a little of that, wanting that such and such should happen. These are our main worries. To free our consciousness, which is bogged down in petty worries, the *sutra* says, " *udyamao bhairavah.*"

When we put in our best efforts, we do not worry whether or not our work will be successful. What does worry mean? It means that we have not worked to the best of our ability. Imagine that you are playing football or running a race. If you put in your full energy, you will have no regrets. If you do not put in your 100 percent, then you may think, "Oh! I could have done better." A person who gives his full efforts knows, "How could I have done better? I did my best and am prepared to accept the results. If I get the fruits I will be fine, and if not, then too I will be happy." When you completely apply your energy, fully using actions, speech and mind, you become *Bhairava*, full. *Bhairava* means fullness.

Dissatisfaction, unhappiness and discontent enter the mind when there is no fullness. Until people find fullness, they cannot have peace, comfort or sleep. At every stage in life, if something is missing, then boredom, uneasiness and discontentment set in.

Just to rid themselves of discontentment, people visit temples and other places of worship. Why do we listen to discourses? Why do people pray? Why do we break a coconut at temples? Is it not to get rid of discontentment and to find contentment, to move from imperfection to perfection? A thirsty person looks for water and a hungry person for food. A person with a full stomach does not look around on either side of the road for a restaurant; only a hungry person does that. Only a person who is building a house will look for a hardware store. Before that, though he walked up and down the road so many times he did not notice the hardware store. An exception is clothing and jewelry stores, which always get noticed except by people whose minds are happy and content. They do not think of them, even for a moment.

Do not think that your mind is fickle or weak. It is not fickle; it merely desires completeness and is roaming here and there looking for completeness. When one is content, then the mind automatically becomes serene and quiet.

The whole of life is a struggle to find contentment. You will never find contentment in any object or any situation. Your very nature is contentment. In order to realise that, you should exert your full effort. Do you know what happens to your body when *rajas*, or restlessness, increases? It does not allow you to sit quietly, at ease. Instead, you fidget, rustle about, squirm, move your legs and tap the table. Sitting in the lawn you pluck the grass and pull leaves from bushes – playing like a monkey! This happens because of *rajas*, unsatisfied physical and mental powers. So to satisfy them we must do some activity.

Some people think that just by sitting quietly, meditation will happen, but it is not the case. Only the person who works well can sit to meditate. There is a misconception that it is the idle people who meditate, pray and sing to God. An idle person can never meditate. In fact, the person who works hard can meditate better. This does not apply to those who over-work themselves. Some people work all day and night like mad-men. They end up over-sleeping or falling asleep even when they sit to meditate. A person who works well, in moderation, can meditate well.

If you have lots of ambition and dynamism, but do not utilise it correctly or in the right direction, then that energy becomes *rajasic*. If we are tired or disturbed, then that *rajas* becomes worry, unless we utilise it in some activity. Good sleep and work increase our *sattvic* nature, and when *sattva* increases we can meditate better. *Sattva* rises when *tamas*, laziness and boredom, vanish. So to make the mind cheerful and peaceful, we need to balance *tamas* and *rajas*. *Rajas* gets subdued when you use 100 percent of your energy in any effort. *Rajas* drives you to activity, and once that activity is finished, the mind changes to its *sattvic* nature. *Tamas* also gets subdued by this use of energy.

Say that on a day off, you decide to work less and to sleep a couple of hours extra or that after a delicious lunch you take a nap. Later, when you wake up, your body feels heavy. The more you sleep, the more you gain weight and feel lazy and the more *rajas* increases. That is the reason one should sleep moderately. Sometimes when you wake up, the mind is pure. At that time, *sattva* is dominant and one easily meditate. To raise the level of *sattva*, put in 100 percent efforts.

"*Udyamao bhairavah*" – "*Bhairava*" means he who nourishes and who creates fullness. *Bhairava* fills up our incompleteness or lack. When we invest 100 percent of our energy in any action, there will be no regrets, and when there are no regrets there is no fear or anxiety. The mind is complete, awake and in the present moment. In this state of awakened consciousness, you again return to: "*Namah śhrī śhambhave…*" "*Namah*" – the mind turns inward, becomes peaceful and surrenders. The surrendered mind finds *śri*, strength, peace, cheerfulness and success. "*ānanda vapuśe*" – happiness spreads around us. We reach our goal and have no need for the *Shiva Sutras*.

Never say, "It will happen if God wishes." This is not the correct way. The good ideas that you have, come from God, so put them into action. We generally run away from effort. There is a saying in Sanskrit: "*udyoginah purusasimha mupaitim lakshmīh*," meaning, "Wealth and prosperity is due only to those who put in their full efforts." Lazy people do not find wealth. God has given everyone hands, and it is up to you as to how you use them. If you want to play sitar, then you have to practice, or if you want to type on a computer you have to learn how. Practice or study is required for anything you want to do.

Effort and continual practice are required in both worldly and spiritual matters. Some people say, "I will go on a pilgrimage when God desires," or "I will go for *sadhana* only if *Guruji* makes me go." This happens only when the mind is not firm and is wavering in its commitment. You do not apply the same rule to other areas. For instance, you do not say, "I will eat only if God feeds me," or "I will see the movie only if God shows it." Only by working hard and applying full effort can you experience good *samadhi*. A lazy person never reaches *samadhi*. Therefore, *satsang*, *sadhana*, and *seva*, all three are very important. When you do these, you enter into yourself, into *śivatattva*. Then it becomes easy to experience love and knowledge.

We treat our wishes and God's wishes differently. We accept things according to our convenience. When you succeed in something, you say, "I won by putting in my full effort," but if you lose you say, "What can be done? It is God's will." You never admit that you did not put in your effort 100 percent.

Actually, God did it; otherwise it would not have happened, even if you tried. So, God alone does everything. This is important to understand- the efforts that you make are also *Shiva*. If God alone is the doer and nothing exists except for him, then he is also enjoying the fruit of action. If God has made you a thief, then through you God will also experience punishment in jail. Suppose you overeat and say, "I have a stomach ache," how is it possible that you have a stomach ache? The aching stomach is God's. If you are not the doer, then you are not the enjoyer of actions either. Remember that he is the doer and also the enjoyer.

You will not get results if you merely keep thinking about a work that you have no interest in doing. If you want to do something, do it 100% and complete it, and if you want to leave a project, then drop it and drop it in your mind too. Whatever you do, do it 100 percent. It is not right to say, "Why should I do it if everything is being done by God?" Only God is doing everything, and he is doing work through you. The God in you is eager to work. Therefore, allow God to work; why do you stop God mid-way?

This is only acceptable when you feel God Himself is stopping mid-way. If you sit and start wondering about it, you will wind up utterly confused. Come out of it, and let your mind be empty.

The energy you have to do work is *Shiva*. Your faults also belong to Him. Virtues and happiness come from knowledge while flaws and misery come from ignorance. If happiness and misery are the same to you, then knowledge and ignorance are the same. You will not feel anger or hatred towards anyone. Liberated and pure, you will march towards the Self. "*Sukhe dukhe samāikatvā lābhāh ālabhau jayājayāt*" – *Krishna* tells *Arjuna*, "Treating with equanimity happiness and misery, gain and loss, victory and defeat, fight the war." Fight without feverishness.

Look at your actions as a witness. The heart beats, blood flows, breath moves in and out, digestion and other functions continue. These processes happen on their own. Even thoughts appear by themselves. Realise that there is no distinction between a complete doer and a complete observer. Then you will become the doer of everything. This should happen naturally.

You should still act. Do not be without doing. The rain falls only when it is time to rain, and the sun rises and sets in its own time. You cannot affect these, but when the sun shines, open the windows. Only then can the rays of sunlight enter. If you open the windows at twelve midnight expecting the sunlight to enter, how can it happen? If the windows are shut it will be dark inside even if the sun is shining. Nature is giving you everything, but still you should put in your full effort. Without effort, you cannot prosper. Only when you apply effort will you get results.

We do not just need physical effort, but also mental and intellectual effort. Some people say, "We did our work with 100 percent effort, but still we faced difficulties. Why do only good people experience misery while bad people are happy?" There is no misery for good people, but if a good man doing good work is foolish and because of this encounters difficulties, it cannot be helped. Just being good is not enough; there should be cleverness with it. Yoga is another name for such a skill. *Krishna* said to *Arjuna*, "*yoga karmasu kauśalam*" – "if you do your work skillfully, then it will bear good results."

Why is skill needed? Skill is not needed to be unhappy. Skill is needed only to avoid misery. Yoga and *sadhana* are the path to overcome misery. Yoga does not only mean physical postures. When you are surrounded by light, there is no question of darkness. Where is misery when you are drowning in joy? Where is poverty if you are rich inside?

So never say, "I will do *sadhana* only when God asks me to do it," or "I will meditate only when *Guruji* makes me meditate." Has *Guruji* not invited you? Does God not want you to do *sadhana*? God is shouting at the top of his voice. All the *rishis* from *Maharishi Vyasa's* time are calling to you in one loud voice, inviting you! They have spoken so many times, "Move ahead! Wake up! Stand up!" We say, "Let it happen if God wishes," only when we do not want to act.

If you want to do something good, do it immediately, but if you want to do something bad, brush it aside. Once when I was in Canada for a *satsang*, two and a half hours after the *satsang*, at 12:30 in the night, an elderly Indian lady came. One of the volunteers asked her to return the next morning, but she insisted and started knocking on my door, demanding, "I need to see *Guruji* right now." I came out and asked her, "What's the matter?" She said, "I have decided to donate $200 to children." I said, "OK, but why the great hurry? It is past mid-night, and you have come from so far in the middle of the night when you could have donated it tomorrow or the day after. I will be here for some time. Why did you come so late?" She said, "*Guruji*, I can't trust my own mind. Today I feel like giving, so I am giving right now." Then, at 1 a.m. she narrated a story to me. She said, "*Guruji*, I would like to tell you a story." I replied, "OK, tell me the story. Anyway, I am awake now." She started:

"A trader was going to Kashi by boat. On the way, his boat started sinking. He saw a fisherman on a nearby boat and asked him to take him aboard and save him. He told the fisherman that otherwise he would drown and die. And that if he took him aboard, then he would give him all his property. The fisherman agreed. Once the boat started moving safely towards the shore, the trader regained his senses and started repenting for having offered all his property to the fisherman. Then he told the fisherman that although he was ready to give him all his property, his wife would not agree to it, so he would only give him half of it, as he had to give the other half to his wife and family. For that he was helpless, as they also needed the property."

"The fisherman kept silent and continued rowing towards the shore. Then the trader wondered why he had offered him half his property. What great thing had he done by saving him from the river? It is his duty to ferry people across, and after all protecting others is only humane. He was just doing his duty and would have committed a sin if had he not saved him. He had actually protected the fisherman from committing a sin. So he told the fisherman he would only give him a quarter of his property. The fisherman did not make a sound. Then, when they reached the shore, the trader gave him a five rupee coin, but the fisherman said that he did not need his money. Shocked, the trader insisted, 'No, no, you take this. Have tea for yourself and get some biscuits for your children.'"

Then the elderly woman said, "*Guruji*, such is the game of the mind. If one has to do some good work, it is best to do it immediately or else one keeps postponing it and never does it. That is why I have come in the middle of the night."

The mind is such that if we have to scold someone we pick up the phone right away and shout at him without caring what time of day or night it is. You may not be aware if the person on the other end of the phone is listening or not! He may have hung up, but once you have shouted you are at peace. The mind wants to do bad things right away.

The energy in you that moves you to act, also will lead you to a state where you are a witness and do not even desire to act. Consciousness blossoms when you are a witness. Then even amidst all your actions consciousness will continue to blossom. So drop all your concepts and put in your full efforts – *"udyamao bhairavah."* Suppose you are unable to do this because of weakness, or you do put in your 100 percent, but restlessness increases. The next *sutra* says:

शक्तिचक्रसंधाने विश्वसंहारः

Śhakti chakra sandhāne viśhvasamhārah

When you direct your attention to your energy centers, the world that you have created disappears.

The question arises- If one rises to a higher position only by hard work, does this justify all those workers and businessmen who work continuously, sweating it out, night and day? And for what purpose? Some Profit? Do they find only profit by working so hard? Sometimes blood pressure rises or ulcers appear, or the world overwhelms them, and anger and hatred begin. By working only to fulfill desires, you invite things that are undesired. When we look around and feel that others have more than what we have, life fills with jealousy. Look at the jealousy in our schools- children say, "She got higher marks than me, and even though we wrote the same answer, she came first while I came third." Or if the person sitting next to you looks and smiles and has a conversation with a person sitting on the other side of you, then it is enough for you to become shocked and uncomfortable.

This world is in our own mind! We look only at the world that exists in our mind, which we imagine in our own way, though the world outside may be different. 70 percent of the problems in our life start because of our imagination. If you are unhappy or have had an unpleasant life, it is due to the world in your mind. You have created such a universe.

"*Viśhva*" is a wonderful word – "*śhva*" means either yesterday or tomorrow, and "*viśhva*" means the special yesterday or tomorrow that we create in our own mind. In our mind, we imagine certain things as huge, though we are uncertain how they actually are. We are stuck in worries about yesterday and imaginings about tomorrow, which is why we lack enthusiasm. Enthusiasm is a quality of life, yet some people find only boredom and unhappiness. Observe, in what direction is your life moving- day by day, are you gaining enthusiasm or losing it?

Look at a child five or six years old or a toddler of three to six months. They are filled with enthusiasm. It overflows from every cell of their body. Compare children with grown-ups and see if enthusiasm increases or decreases with age. Are we really living when we lose enthusiasm?

From the age of twenty, we started to slowly die. Today, this starts at fifteen. Dying starts as soon as you lose enthusiasm, and life is over by the time we reach the age of fifty. Although there is no enthusiasm left in life, still we call it life! Today, college students have no enthusiasm. They have already grown old, and have lost their enjoyment of life. After the television age started in India, people began maturing very quickly and now life passes very fast.

The people of the last two or three generations were so enthusiastic even at fifty, sixty or seventy years of age. They are not totally gone, but if you observe the majority of people in schools, colleges and towns, very few of them have cheerful expressions. Instead, they rush about with long faces, frowning. Why lead such a life? Or look at the people who visit temples. Some of them are so fearful that they tremble, while others walk with scrunched eyebrows. People with cheerful faces are rarely seen. This has happened because of our "*Viśhva*" – we have made such a world. Now to drop this, should you run away from society to some cave in the Himalayas? You will not find happiness just by entering a cave. The world originates in your mind. Only you have created it, and only you can drop it. The solution is in your own body.

"Śhakti chakra sandhāne viśhvasamhārah" – there are different types of centers in your body. Bring your attention to these centers, observe them and the world of worries and thoughts that trouble your mind will disappear. There will be peace. This is a very important *sutra*. When we feel anger, emotion or excitement, then different parts of our body experience various sensations. When you get angry, the area between the two eyebrows ignites; when you become unhappy, the throat starts to choke; when you feel hatred, a sensation happens in the heart region. What happens when you feel jealous? The stomach churns. Goodwill is also generated in the stomach. For example, we say, "I had a hearty laugh," and when one feels very happy the area around the navel experiences some sensations. Similarly, when we feel jealousy or love, there is a sensation around the heart. Likewise, when you are sad there is a feeling in the throat and also when you want to express gratitude, you cannot express it in words, and we often say that the throat chokes. All together in our body there are seven *chakras*, or energy centers, and all 27,000 subtle nerves in our body are connected to these seven centers.

The first center is *mūladhāra chakra*. Here, the energy is either dormant or active. Bring your attention to this center. All through our lives, though we have a body we do not place our attention on it or even observe it. Our body is a wonder! Do you know our body is like a city with millions of living organisms inside? Some are our friends, and some are our enemies. Your intestines holds

50,000 different types of bacteria, which are all helpful. We call the body "*purusha*," meaning "those who live in a city," because the body is like a city.

Shakti, or energy, rises from *mūladhāra chakra* to *svādhihthāna chakra* where it expresses itself either as lust or creativity. When it climbs up higher to *manipūra chakra*, the region around the navel, it is expressed as jealousy, generosity, joy or greed. Usually, a rich man's stomach is depicted to be large and round, and often it is like that. Generosity, happiness and greed all happen in this one place. The same energy rises to the heart, *anahata chakra*, where it expresses itself in three ways- love, hatred and fear. When you are frightened, you place your hand on your heart, and also when you express love or respect, you touch your heart. Feelings of hatred are also connected to the heart.

Then the same energy rises to the throat region, or *viśuddha chakra*, where it expresses itself as gratitude or misery. When you feel grief or express gratitude, the throat begins to choke. This energy then travels upward to the area between the eye-brows, known as *ajña chakra,* where it is expressed as awareness, knowledge and anger. So *Shiva*'s third eye represents both knowledge and anger. When *Shiva* is angry he reduces everything to ashes just by opening his third eye. Finally, when this same energy rises to the top of the head to *sahaswara chakra*, there is only bliss and joy.

This is how the energy of consciousness travels, and you can become familiar with it by observing this movement. Normally, life energy is flowing through these *chakras*, but if we feel under pressure or disturbed, then knots form in the *chakras,* obstructing the flow of energy. Place your attention on the energy in these *chakras*, and you will see that the negative energy in the *chakras* gradually dissolves. All impurities disappear, and positive qualities are established. If you feel jealous and then meditate with attention on your navel, the jealousy will automatically subside. Due to jealousy, we make mistakes and then try to defend ourselves by justifying what we did. We should know that all that happened was because of impurities in our *chakras*.

"Shakti chakra sandhāne viśhvasamhārah" – the world will be annihilated if you come in contact with these *chakras* through meditation. "Annihilating the world" means dropping the worries of this world forever. A classic example of losing the world is when you fall asleep. If you kept worrying about issues of the world you could never sleep. After all, what is sleep? You can only sleep when you are alone. If you keep your world with you, constantly thinking about different things, you will never be able to sleep. You will stay awake, tossing and turning.

You can move beyond this by meditating on the energy centers. During the advanced course the energy centers are dealt with. Everyone should take out three to four days every six months or a year to do an advanced course. When we spend time in silence, meditating, the body and mind become pure, quiet and full of enthusiasm. Many people have experienced this after doing an advanced course.

Although *chakras* exist in the body, do not imagine that they are like wheels on a cart or "*Ashok chakra*." There are no such *chakras* in the body. Do not think like this. The moment you start visualizing it like this, fantasies increase. In India, it is said that there is a lotus with so many petals at one place in the body and at another place in the body there is a lotus having another number of petals; this is because we love flowers. While we use the phrase "like a flower" to describe anything that is continually fresh and tender, there are really no such lotuses in the body. We notice this only when our mind becomes delicate and subtle.

For a computer to work properly, it needs to stay at the right temperature and be in proper condition. Our body is a super-computer, which is very delicate. If a man-made computer requires a specific environment, then what do we need? Our bodies also require proper conditions. That is to say the mind should be alert and aware, and the body should stay fit and active, which requires regular *pranayama*, exercise and so forth. When you do *pranayama*, do it will full awareness and attention – "*udyamao bhairavah*" When you work hard, only then can you enjoy rest, and that rest is where *shivtattva* is.

"*Shakti chakra sandhāne viśhvasamhārah*" – when you direct your attention to the energy centers, the world gets annihilated. You yourself have to take apart your own world. Nobody else can do it because you are responsible for creating your own world. There is a story about a very famous locksmith. It was said that nobody could make a lock that could be compared with his locks. One night when he was with the king, thieves came, put them in handcuffs and robbed them both. The king said, "Anyway, since you are with me, there's no problem." In the morning, the locksmith looked at the locks on the handcuffs and started crying. He told the king, "I made this lock, and I never do a second-rate job. So nobody can pick open this lock, and even breaking them open will be hard!"

In this world, we wear shackles of our own making. Nobody else has chained you with shackles. You are responsible for it. Wake up. Look at your world – what is there? Through your work, what great thing are you achieving? We work merely to sustain life, but we feel as though we are doing it for some noble purpose. This is an illusion.

Your whole life you struggle, just to earn a little money, but when it comes to the Divine, you say, "It will happen if God wants it." To achieve something in this world, you wear yourself out and do not let up, even if it leaves you gasping for breath, but when it comes to inquiring into your self or doing *sadhana*, you say, "Let it happen as God wishes." Only for that do you need God's blessings? However, in this world, you receive what is yours only because of *prarabdha karma*, or results of past actions, not just by your work or efforts. Your *prarabdha karma* results in all the conveniences you enjoy in your life – pleasures, facilities, comforts, house and so on, while your own efforts guarantee greater awareness and lead to higher states of consciousness. Yet we do everything backwards. We are ready to wear ourselves out for some desire in the world, but for meditation, we say, "I will do it when God wishes." This is the world we create.

The whole world is a *shakti chakra*, an energy center. Look at it from a fresh perspective. What is this world but energy? What is this body? It is energy! Every atom in the body is energy. Energy is produced every day after we take food, and that energy goes back to the world. All the elements are energy. The energy cycle keeps going on. The ocean water evaporates and falls as rain; rain water falls into the river, which returns to the sea. In this way the cycle continues. The body converts the food we eat into human waste, which goes back into to the soil, where it acts as fertiliser for plants, flowers, fruits and nuts, which we then eat, and the cycle goes on.

The body is also made up of the five elements and when it dies, it turns back to soil again. Even in the body such a cycle is going on. Everything is recycled. The whole world is like a big recycling machine where everything gets reused. Look at air- the air we breathe out goes to trees and plants, and then the oxygen from them returns to us and the cycle continues. The whole world has only a fixed amount of air and water circulating, and it is the same story for every other element. Even for soil, this holds true. The soil has been the same throughout the ages; no new soil is produced. The world cannot have anything new, not even a small sesame seed. Even scientists say the same in the law of conservation of matter and energy, which explains that matter and energy are inter-convertible and that matter can be neither destroyed nor recreated.

In this way the whole world is one *shakti chakra*. Your life will end in forty to sixty years. After that, the breath, mind and soul of this life will be recycled into a new body, which will also die and be recycled. Everything in this world has a cycle. Whether a dog, cat, parrot, crow, or owl, all die only to be born as some other species in another womb. This recycling is also known as *punarjanma*, or rebirth.

This world is a wheel made up of different wombs. You are now born as a human, maybe a man or woman. A rat may be born as a cat and the cat as some other creature. Understand that you take rebirth in the form that you adore, hate or fear. The rat, which is afraid of the cat, dies with a cat impressed on its memory, and will be reborn as a cat. The cat hates the dog and so will be reborn as a dog. If a dog fears man, it will take rebirth as a man. Humans are the only creature that scares everything. In this century, we see different types of people, some like tigers and others like crows, snakes and so on. We also give the name "Nagraj"- king of the snakes. It is not their fault if they are like snakes. Snakes are very scared of people and people of snakes.

"*Shakti chakra sandhāne viśhvasamhārah*" – look at the world from another point of view- as a large wheel full of infinite energy. The moment you realise that everything is changing, your mind becomes pleasant and returns to "*svātmānanda prakāśa vapuśe.*" Knowing this, let us come back to the *Shiva Sutras*. Practice this awareness as an experiment- like the *shakti chakras*, everything in this world is changing.

Here in India, people visit temples and apply sacred ash. Devotees of *Shiva* apply ash in three stripes all over the body, especially on forehead, cheeks, neck and abdomen. Sometimes people do not know why and so they say, "My father applied them, so I also apply them," or "I apply it because it was offered in the temple." We apply ash as a symbol of *Shiva*, of auspiciousness. Ash indicates that the skin, or body, will return to ash. It is only a question of time. This understanding helps you become detached from the world in your mind. Understand the ultimate truth while applying ash because the ash alone is real. When we look for permanence in impermanent objects, we find only misery.

Today, a young boy came, he was in love with a young woman. The couple swore to each other, "We will stay together forever." Later, it became known that the boy had been with some other girl for five or six days, and they had been to a movie together. Both of them became disturbed. The young woman demanded to know why he had not confessed this earlier and accused him of cheating. The relationship ended. There was no question of staying together forever or of being made for each other.

"*Shakti chakra sandhāne viśhvasamhārah*" – let us not search for permanence in impermanent objects. Ash reminds you that everyone will eventually die. A person with a bank balance of ten lakhs and someone with only ten rupees, both will die one day. You have created this world. Only you can come out of it. The entire creation is a *shakti chakra.* Understand this truth and keep it close to you. Then there will be no more duality in the mind and- "*svātmānanda prakāśa vapuśe.*"

BUBBLES ON THE WATER

Are you awake, sleeping or are you dreaming? The problem is that you are doing both. While you think you are awake, you are actually dreaming. We do not notice the differences between the waking and dreaming states. That is why we try to make our dreams come true. To consider dreams real is a sign of ignorance.

Look at a child who starts crying after he wakes up from a dream. He thinks that the dog that was chasing him in his dream was real, and so even after waking up he keeps crying and shouting, saying that a dog bit him. While considering a dream as real is a sign of ignorance, understanding that reality is just like a dream is a sign of an enlightened person. The main problem lies in not understanding the difference. Instead, you sit, day-dreaming. There are two types of dreams- a day-dream happens when we are awake, and dream happens when we are sleep.

When you become aware that a thief has broken into your house, fear makes you wake up. Or imagine you have lost your way home, you are alone at night and there are no streetlights.

The heart starts beating faster, and you can clearly hear the sound of each beat of the heart. Until that moment, you are not aware that you have a heart. At these moments are you really awake?

जाग्रत्स्वप्नसुषुप्तभेदे तुर्याभोगसंभवः
Jāgrat svapna susuptabhede tūryābhogasambhavah

The three states of consciousness are the awakened state, the dream state and the state of deep sleep. Only when one distinguishes between these states can one experience the fourth state.

We should understand this next *sutra* clearly. In life, we are not aware of the differences between the three states of consciousness, waking, dreaming and deep sleep. Everything looks the same in the dark! *Advaitins*, or non-dualists, and *Dvaitins*, or dualists, each give their own view. *Advaitins* say that everything is one and the same, and *Dvaitins* reply that yes, everything looks the same in the dark. Only in light can you distinguish differences. We need to understand this science of difference.

Right now, you are seated on the floor, listening to me. Are you aware of the difference between your body and the floor? Experience it right this moment. Are you experiencing the contact of your body with the floor? Do you notice the difference? Similarly, do you feel the difference between your body and the clothes you are wearing? Become aware of it now. Do you feel the shirt making contact with your skin? Only then you will know that the shirt and body are actually different. While engaged in different activities, observe the difference between mind and intellect, mind and breath, breath and body, body and ground and so on. Try to become aware of the difference between the states of waking, dreaming and sleep. This is the science of differentiation. We will know if we are asleep, dreaming or awake once we understand this science.

However, we are like a drunken man or a monkey. Our waking state is not wakeful at all. We act like a monkey that has been forced to drink alcohol and then eat asafetida. In moments when you feel afraid or when your life is in danger, you wake up fully and become aware of everything around you. A beginner cyclist spots each and every rock in the road, and as he sees rocks, he shouts, "Rock! Rock," and then in mid-fall, he yells, "Falling, falling!" If someone who is afraid of cockroaches gets out of bed, switches on the light and glimpses even a small cockroach, he will scream! He imagines it is a big cockroach. However, at that moment he is really awake. Similarly, if a person sees a snake, it is the worst. He might even faint.

We are not aware of the differences between the waking state, dreaming state and sleeping state. When we get up in the morning, our eyes look drowsy. After having breakfast, we go out to work with sleepy eyes, and in that very condition all work gets done. If someone has a *masala dosa* or some other heavy food for breakfast before going to class, you can understand his condition. We find 75 percent of students are asleep or dreaming, especially if the subject is history or geography. They are all imagining that they are competing in the Olympics or sitting in some cinema or somewhere else.

"*Jāgrat svapna susupti*" – if we understand the differences between these three states, then we will be able to experience the fourth state of consciousness – "*tūryābhogasambhavah.*" We can realise the fourth state of consciousness in between waking and dreaming or in between deep sleep and waking. It is called "the fourth state"; they have not named it. It is the state where the mind is awake though the body is resting, and you know you are present, but do not know where you are. This is meditation: I know I am meditating, and I am not dreaming or doing something else. It is not the waking state, dream state or even the state of deep sleep.

If you start to enter that state where you are not dreaming or sleeping, you start to enter the state of *samādhi*, where you will be free from worries and have a sense of innocence. So where should you search for *Śhivatattva*? Search for it in between the states of waking and dreaming, not far away in Mount Kailash. In the moments right after you wake up, but are not yet fully awake, close your eyes and start to meditate. At that time, the mind is free from worries and the thought process. This is "*chaitanyamātmā*." You will begin to experience the fourth state of consciousness, which lies in between the other three.

The consciousness and enthusiasm expressed in a new-born baby are missing in a very learned person. The *ātmā*, Self, is nothing but consciousness. This quality of consciousness gradually reduces with education. Why is that? Are we really living or do we only seem to be? Our smile has disappeared, and we lead a mechanical existence. It is said that a child laughs 400 times a day, a youth just seventeen times and an adult does not even laugh. Professors not only do not laugh, but they make laughter an offence!

What is a sign of consciousness? It is our enthusiasm, joy and creativity. Even if you cause some problems for others or make mischief, it does not matter. Keep doing something. Mischief is also a sign of consciousness. Where there is consciousness, there is no laziness. Do not sit around moping. That indicates a lack of consciousness.

ज्ञानं जाग्रत्

Jñānam jāgratah

The knowledge of the external world is available only in the waking state.

The definition of the waking state is given in this *sutra*. Many of us do not wake up in order to experience the world. Although the eyes are open and the ears listening, the mind is somewhere else. Such a state is not the waking state.

स्वपनोविकल्पाः

Svapno vikalpāh

The dream state is where the thoughts are present and we have no awareness of outside world.

Dream means *vikalpa*. At night, you can see the stars, but once the sun comes up you cannot see the stars. They are still there, but you cannot see them because the sun is shining. We are dreaming while we are awake, but we do not see it as a dream. While we are sleeping we feel it is a dream because we are not aware of the outside world. Even without the awareness of outside things, dreams continue inside, just like the stars seen in the sky at night. While dreaming, things that we experienced before automatically appear.

When we say "*vikalpa*," what does it mean? When the mind keeps on thinking about objects it does not want to think about, we call it *vikalpa*. In the mind, there is only one *sankalpa* and all other thoughts are *vikalpa*. "*Sankalpa*" means the mind's decision to do something after careful examination. "*Vikalpa*" means thinking uselessly about objects. Analyse if you have more *vikalpa* in your mind or more *sankalpa*. There is 98 percent *vikalpa*. *Vikalpa* creates disturbance. Dreams mean *vikalpa*, and *vikalpa* drains energy from the mind.

We dream when we are not in the present and struggling either with the past or the future. We do not understand things as they are. "*Vikalpa*" means to think about an object differently from how it actually is. It is an illusion. We need to come out of this dream. Only then our life will be *jāgrit,* or awake, and we will be happy.

Those who dream will never have happiness. Not only do we dream for ourselves, but we also dream on others' behalf. We have hundreds of dreams in our head and not just one. "*Jāgrit svapna susupti tūryābhoga sambhavah.*"

अविवेको मायासौषुप्तम्

Aviveko māyā sausuptam

The state of deep sleep is lack of discrimination and of awareness.

When you are asleep and are not aware of anything, that is "*māyā*"; "*māyā*" is not being of aware of anything.

त्रितयमोक्ता वीरेशः

Tritaya bhoktā vīreśhah

A brave man enjoys the three states of waking, dreaming and sleep with detachment.

Your life is a long sleep in which you talk, toss and turn. Sometimes, children fall sleep before taking milk, and so the mother wakes them up to feed them, and then they fall sleep again. They might not even remember this happened. Like this, your life is a long slumber, in which you are awake for a very short time. Then you turn to your other side and fall asleep under the blankets again. When parents wake their children up for Saturday morning school, the certain reply is, "Let me sleep for a few more minutes." It is the same story with everyone. Some wake up early on their own, while the majority continue to doze throughout life, promising to wake up soon. A lack of discrimination due to *māyā* is a sign that one is sleeping.

"*Aviveko māyā sausuptam*" – what is sleep? It is not being aware of the present situation, or *aviveka*. In sleep, no learning happens. Instead, we repeat mistakes over and over again. We do not make new mistakes, which we can learn from, but instead repeat the same old mistakes over and over again. This is *aviveka*, the work of *māyā*.

Your whole life, you are constantly using your mind to imagine things as they are not. Most of the time, you worry about others' opinions about you, but do other people have time to think about you? Day in and day out you worry about your honour and reputation.

A lady was telling everyone, "My son is a good boy, and he wouldn't disobey us in any matter." That boy married a girl from a different caste against the will of his parents. This lady was constantly thinking about what others thought, and after the surprise of her son's act, what happened? She could appear before others and so she locked herself inside her home. She thought that she could not go to other marriages because people would ask about her son's inter-caste marriage. She cried, "My pride, my honour, my respect – all lost!" It was not just for one or two days, but for a whole year that she could not leave the house! She kept worrying about what others would say and think about her. So I told her, "When do others have time to think about you? And seeing you, even if they do say something, why should you get upset?" This is called *māyā*.

We constantly worry about what others think about us, but everyone's ideas and opinions are short-lived. They are momentary. Suppose someone thinks that you are a good person. How long will it take him to change his mind about you? It will take just a matter of seconds. They may label you as bad; many people may think you are bad. How much time will it take to change their opinions also? The opinions of others are like bubbles on the water. If we depend on them, we cannot live at all. Can such a life be steady? There is a saying: "Building castles in the air." It is *māyā*, foolishness, to lead life dependent on others' opinions.

We see the world every day, but without learning anything new. There is no discrimination. Many people have been born and have also left this world. Many are dying, and we will also die one day. We intentionally remain ignorant of this fact. This is *māyā*; it is absence of discrimination, simply staying asleep.

"*Aviveko māyā sausuptam tritaya bhoktā vīreśah*" – knowing this much is enough. Once you know that everything is *māyā,* a lack of discrimination, *māyā* disappears. The air bubble below the water's surface disappears as soon as it rises to the surface. Recognising *māyā* as *māyā* is discrimination. Knowing that everything in this world is changing is discrimination, but we do not grasp this because we are sleeping. As soon as we are aware we are sleeping, we instantly wake up. There is only one answer to some questions, and the reply, whether it is "yes" or "no," has only one meaning. If you ask a sleeping person whether or not he is asleep, a "yes" has no meaning. Even if he says, "no," it also means he is not asleep, and if he says, "yes," it really means no. Similarly, whatever reply you receive for certain questions, the meaning remains the same. The moment you wake up and understand *māyā,* you are free from *māyā* and return to "*ātmā chaitanya*," to "*śhrī śhambhave svātmānanda prakāśa vapuśe*."

When we realise that we made a mistake, we repent. Do you know what happens when we repent? We get angry, we blame ourselves, and not only do we blame ourselves, we blame others too. When there is a fire in your belly, only then can the heat be experienced outside. The insults flying out of your mouth only show the external heat, but the fire inside is not seen. You feel angry at yourself because you feel: "I have not learnt anything. I couldn't move forward in life despite my best efforts." You feel frustrated with yourself. That is why the *sutra* says to be brave, "*tritaya bhoktā vīreśah*."

The path is complex and difficult. You may fail one hundred times before you succeed. Do not lose hope or become disheartened. Ultimately, if you are ready to triumph, you will, but for that you need to be *vīreśah*, one who is ready to accept failure. People think the opposite, that only one who is unwilling to accept defeat will triumph. This is totally incorrect. A person who accepts defeat will become peaceful. Those who do not accept defeat boil inside with a fire of revenge.

It is hard to say that people with seething, disturbed intellects can really achieve success. If they find any success, it is only outside, and in their hearts they know that they have lost. Only people who accept defeat can be brave! One who says, "I have lost," can be cool, without vengeance. The peaceful mind is courageous, but a disturbed mind cannot have courage.

"*Tritaya bhoktā vīreśah*" – we have enjoyed neither *yoga*, union, nor *bhoga*, enjoyment. We can be content either in *yoga* or *bhoga*, but we have not even enjoyed *bhoga*, the enjoyments in our life. Look at the face of a child eating a lollipop. He enjoys it fully, and his face glows happily. He is so content! Now look at people eating in restaurants like cows – do they find contentment there? Is there enthusiasm? No. However, suppose you sing a song to a child, it will intently listen before falling asleep, immersed in the song. Even asleep, the face remains cheerful, and the moment it gets up, you see innocence, happiness, love and contentment on the child's face. Even after a complete sleep, you get up without any expression at all on your face, and you start grumbling. Even if you get more sleep, will you find contentment, happiness or satisfaction on the face? You only get out of bed only because it is necessary.

Look at the faces of newlyweds. There may be happiness for one or two days, and that too before the marriage. Afterwards, there is only fear, apprehension, worries and problems. Are they content? Does contentment come through enjoyment? There would not be so much violence in the world if contentment came with *bhoga*, enjoyment. People who do acts of violence are searching only for contentment. But do you find any glow on their faces, any happiness or any contentment? There are people who are constantly engaging in pleasure. Be careful of such people. Are they *yogis* or great *bhogis*?

Now take the case of politicians. Are they happy and satisfied? They are far, far away from happiness. They are far away even from the word. And contentment, they will understand this word maybe after seven more lifetimes. Also, when you look at many saints, *sadhus*, *mahātmas* and *tathāgatās*, is there contentment in their eyes or peace on their faces? They have greed for power, money, success, for having lots of devotees, in them. What is the meaning of greed? Greed means one has not properly experienced the enjoyments one has had. One who has not properly eaten thinks about food all the time.

The one who experiences the three states of waking, dreaming and sleep is *vīreśah*. In life, there is knowledge, activity and attachment. When you start liking a thing, does the attachment last? After some time, it disappears. Many people worry about forming attachments. Self-realisation happens and anger follows it. The wheel moves on continuously and events follow one after the other.

However lack of discrimination has set in, whatever feelings there are, say lust or anger, the one who can witness them bravely is *vīreśah*. Know this much- "Whether in good times or in bad times, I am not the doer. I am only the witness, while the higher self in me is experiencing. It is not me who sleeps, but the higher self in me." Look at it simply as a detached observer. This is very subtle knowledge. It is possible that some people might take this knowledge in the wrong sense.

Many people create problems for themselves and others. On some holy days, many people fast, subjecting their own bodies to hardship. *Krishna* says in the *Gītā*, "I am also in the body, and you hurt me." This is foolishness! You turn yourself into a demon when you torture the Self present in you, and you become a greater demon when you torture others.

"*Tritaya bhoktā vīreśah*" – to experience we need courage. We can show courage and advise others, but to live a solitary life requires a lot of courage. Only with courage, can you move forward. So we need the *Shiva Sutras*. Take courage and things will start happening. Be patient. Cowardly people never have patience and want things to happen immediately. Once, a lady said, "It is late. I will sleep for five minutes and come back." Is it possible to sleep that quickly? It is just like bathing in a hurry. You may bathe quickly, but half of the body will not even get wet. Another time a youth came and told me, "*Guruji*, I am so ashamed to tell you that I am very lazy in applying soap to my whole body. I use soap on my hands one day, on my legs another day and on my face the third day." At least he had the courage to admit this. He is not the only one; there are many who do this. Some do not even bathe.

"*Tritaya bhoktā vīreśah*" – have courage, patience and forbearance. It is not possible to become fit after only one day of doing exercise, *pranayama* and *yoga asanas*. Similarly, your mind will also not change in one day. It takes time and patience. Your mind has come into its present form over so many years. Now give it some time to change. Do not blame yourself if you fail. Do not feel, "I have done all the courses; for a year I have meditated regularly and done *Sudarshan Kriya*, but still I get angry. I'm useless. There is no point of going to all these courses and *satsangs*." Do not blame yourself and disturb the equilibrium in your own mind or start digging your own grave.

Once, when I was in Ooty, India somebody told me, "There is one very brave saint residing nearby. His specialty is that he has dug his own grave. He is such a great soul that he has given instructions to be buried in the grave he has dug for himself." What do you think? Is he a great soul or is it arrogance? While you are alive, do what you want to do and leave the rest for others to finish after your death. He has not left any work for others. They do not even have the freedom to build his grave because that has to happen according to his wish. He has such a deep-rooted interest in living and the body. There is a feeling that I have done an amazing and shocking feat, which nobody else has dared to do.

Be patient and brave. Do not fall into self-blame. You are different from the you that experiences the three states of waking, dreaming and deep sleep. It takes time to discover this. It does not happen in a day. It will become an experience only when you meditate regularly.

Sometimes while sleeping you become a witness to your own dreams; the ability to witness has awakened in you. Sometimes while you are asleep and the body rests, you realise that you are dreaming – you are just a witness. When you have such an experience, pleasantness, love and affection, which are your own nature, gush through you. If this experience has not yet happened, have patience and be brave. It will happen.

विस्मयो योग भूमिकाः

Vismayo yoga bhūmikāh
Wonder is the basis for union.

It is enough if we understand this *sutra*. Until now, many techniques have been given to unite body, breath, mind and Self, for union to happen and for us to remain in the Self. The technique given now is very important.

Can you accomplish any work without a base or a foundation? Can you build a house without a foundation? Where will it stand? How will the walls be supported? To walk or stand, where do we put our legs? We can do these only thanks to the earth. Even your existence is a wonder. What is that existence? What is the meaning of *yoga*? Where does *yoga* begin? It starts with wonder, *vismayo*.

Have you ever observed a curious child around six months old? A baby examines its hands and fingers with amazement as if though it were seeing something amazing. The baby is just looking at its hand! The moment you attain knowledge without wonder attached to it, that knowledge is worthless. You can even treat such knowledge as ignorance. Only knowledge that creates wonder in you is real knowledge. What we consider as knowledge actually destroys our ability to be amazed. What is left in life when there is no wonder or amazement? Life becomes dull. Wonder is a quality of life, and through wonder we can attain union, *yoga*. Wonder is the basis for *yoga*.

Anything you see around you is amazing. When a child sees a leaf it asks, "Why it is green?" No sooner than you reply, he asks, "Why is the sky blue?", "Why does an elephant have a trunk?" or "Why does a horse not have a trunk?" They may also ask why clouds move in the sky and where they go. Often even parents do not have answers to their questions. Children ask questions and then fall silent. They wonder where they will go if they reach the stars. They think that their father has been there and can tell them about it or that their uncle or brother may know and tell them about it. A child does not know that his elders also do not know and gets silenced by vague answers or a scolding.

Children always wonder. Since birth, it is our nature. It is a sign of life. That is why wonder leads into *yoga*. It is a part of union. Similarly, a genuine scientist who has a scientific attitude will never think that he has learnt everything. There is so much to learn, and real knowledge ignites the curiosity to know even more after having learnt something. However, people who have only partial knowledge gossip and provoke controversy. These people raise all kinds of difficulties and cause trouble. The problems and misfortune that happen in the world are caused by such people.

The people who do not know anything as well as the well-read, knowledgeable people are not responsible for calamities in the world. It is the group of people in-between who cause trouble. They are neither here nor there and pretend to know everything. There never wonder about anything. That is why there is no foundation in them for *yoga* to happen. When you have no sense of wonder and see a leaf, you say, "This is just a leaf. What is there in it to appreciate?" Likewise, you feel why would anyone look at a flower? You will start to wonder only when you see things with a fresh vision. With wonder, *yoga* begins.

Yoga does not mean sitting in a closed room doing *pranayama* or sit-ups till you are gasping for breath. We have misunderstood *yoga*, taking it to mean only certain *asanas* – lifting the legs, lowering the hands, etc. What is meant by *yoga* classes? Is *asana* practice meant only to purify and strengthen the body and eliminate disease? There is no doubt that these benefits do happen, but *yoga* is not just this. A consciousness in wonder is the foundation for *yoga*. Out of this consciousness, innocence is born. Look at the sun at sunset. The sun sets and the moon rises. Look at the sky and sun; nature is filled with wonder. Even the body is such a wonder. Look at the body. How is it created? What are the various types of veins inside? This is really amazing. There are many types of insects in the world. A child will catch hold of an insect, put it in a matchbox and watch it with wonder and delight. This is meditation. This is surrender. We should look at the variety in the world, the many different object, animals, people, insects, etc., with a sense of wonder rather than with a feeling of "I know it all."

There are three types of feelings: "I know," "I do not know" and third, "I cannot know." In Sanskrit these are called "*jñāt*," the known, "*ajñāt*," the unknown, and "*ajñeya*," the unknowable. To approach the unknowable, start wondering about the known and about the unknown. *Yoga* is the unknowable.

While a child who has caught a butterfly is wonderstruck, we are apathetic even if a beautiful wonder is shown to us. You travel to visit the Taj Mahal, glance at it while snacking on peanuts and say, "Oh, is this the Taj Mahal?" Then you start giving your opinion about it or complaining about problems or worries. Did you really see the Taj Mahal? Only a site-seeing ritual has been fulfilled. Others even see the Taj Mahal while sitting in a bus and say, "What is there to see? It is only a marble building." Again, look at children. Take them to a beach or the river, and they will return with their favorite pebbles. You will scold them for bringing back junk, but remember that to them the stones are like silver, gold and pearls – they are happy, excited and filled with enthusiasm over these rocks.

"*Vismayo yoga bhūmikāh*" – the world offers so much variety that leads us to wonder. Sometimes, you feel that God has failed because in spite of so much variety, you still get bored. In fact, if you look, you can find novelty in each and every object in this world. A whole life is not enough time to appreciate these delights. When you feel that something is new, then wonder happens. *Yoga* means to experience this newness and become one with it.

Life is ever changing and ever new. That is why the *sutra* says, "*vismayo yoga bhūmikāh.*" Live your life with wonder. It is very easy, but the capacity to wonder fades as we grow older or when we think that we know everything. So we have to revive this capacity. Look at each moment and every day as new. We have no enthusiasm, and we say, "It's the same *satsang*, same song, same festival, and same exhibition." Even if we repeat something, the capacity to wonder should be limitless.

What is the nature of the unknown in this vastness? You must awaken it within yourself. Look at yourself with wonder. Observe your mind and see how mischievous it is! Is it not enough just to have a mind for you to wonder at? It is not steady, even for a second – the thought that is present one moment is gone the next moment. Some people board a bus from Jayanagar to go to Malleshwaram, get down somewhere in between and decide to return on another bus. These are games the mind plays! Observe the mind with wonder, and you will be happy.

The nature of the mind is such that it grabs onto new things, but quickly tires of them. The mind does not like anything old. Each day it needs new objects, clothes, accessories and places, but the heart is fond of the old. We are proud to introduce someone as "my old friend" or my "longtime friend." We take more pride in old friends than in new ones. We hardly ever introduce new friends to someone. When we discuss relationships, we describe them as how long they have been. A couple of lovers claim, "Our love is ancient," or "Our relationship is from a previous birth." The mind is attracted to the new, but the heart cherishes the old.

Wonder exists where love has been awakened; wonder is part of love. When a baby is born, the parents and elders are so delighted; they describe the baby in detail and take pride in it. The baby's each and every action arouses wonder in them because it is mixed with love. There is wonder in love. When the mind starts to wonder, it becomes quiet and peaceful, and one gets established in the happiness of the Self.

Saints perform miracles to awaken wonder in people. If there were a new miracle every day, people would get used to them, and it would not cause wonder. The saints purposefully resort to miracles to inspire wonder, love and devotion, but it does not always work that way. People look for miracles, but there is no point if people only take interest in miracles and do not start feeling wonder.

When your hunger for knowledge is kindled, you will automatically enter into wonder. When you start a pump, water gushes out of the well, if there is water in the well. Some people pour water from outside if there is no water inside, but the process should start from within. Knowledge ignites the capacity to wonder, and love fills your life with wonder. *Yoga* is possible only when head and heart become one and join with the Self. Then body, breath, mind, memory and ego all merge and move to one rhythm.

Love is ancient, but it does not cause boredom. Nobody says, "This love is so old. I am tired of it." Ancient love is filled with wonder. We recognise the new as inventions and take an interest in them, but not in the old; the new creates wonder in us. It is the wonder that sparks interest. Throughout our lives, we are looking only for something interesting, and that comes with having wonder in each moment.

"Namah śhrī śhambhave svātmānanda prakāśa vapuśe." We start to experience *svātmānanda,* the joy of the Self. Leave everything else. Simply through wonder, the mind will settle into *yoga.*

HONOUR DESIRE

इच्छाशक्तिरुमा कुमारी
icchāśhaktir umā kumārī.

The energy of desire is an unwed maiden.

There is a beautiful story about Kanyakumari, which is at India's southernmost tip. *Shiva* was residing on Mount Kailash, which lies to the far north of India. *Uma* had a desire to marry *Shiva*. *Uma* means *Parvati*, and *Parvati* was a virgin, who was meditating and praying in a place that is now called Kanyakumari. Hearing *Uma*'s prayer, *Shiva* set off from Kailash with his retinue. As per the rules at that time, the marriage had to be finalised before sunrise, or else it could not happen.

However, *Uma* had the power to destroy hosts of demons only if she remained a virgin. All the gods started to worry about how the demons would be destroyed if *Uma* were to marry *Shiva* and go to Kailash; what would be the fate of southern India? So Indra, king of the gods, disguised himself as a rooster and went to the place where *Shiva* and his attendants were resting for the night. In the middle of the night, well before daybreak, he started crowing. Everyone thought that it was dawn because the rooster crows before the sun rises each morning. So *Shiva* and his retinue stopped, thinking that there was no point to go any further for the marriage. There is a place called Suchindrum that is fifty kilometers away from Kanyakumari, and it is believed to be the place where the marriage party stopped while *Parvati* meditated at Kanyakumari. This is the story. *Uma* remained a virgin and stayed at Kanyakumari, and the sun rose while all this happened.

There is a spiritual aspect to this story. The energy of desire leads us to believe that it will make us happy, but in fact it cannot. Even if a desire gets fulfilled, it does not give lasting happiness. So the energy of desire never reaches its goal, which is only for your own benefit. Otherwise, desire cannot remain as an independent energy.

Imagine that the river Ganga originated in Gangotri and terminated in the sea. Then immediately the story would end. However, the river continues flowing. It does not ever reach the sea once and for all. Her desire to merge with the sea is unfulfilled, and as this desire remains unfulfilled, she continues to flow. What is the solution? Since desire is a virgin, she cannot ever meet happiness. Therefore, our ancestors decided to honour the power of desire, *māyā, Uma*'s power. Honour her or else she will never grant happiness. Since desire cannot reach its completion, she cannot give happiness.

When you honour desire, those desires that are necessary get fulfilled and those that are unnecessary fall away. This is the story of Kanyakumari. *Shiva* is not somewhere in Kailash, but has come very close and stopped. The desire was expected to be fulfilled, but stays unfulfilled. There is an important difference between these two positions. Any desire, once fulfilled, takes you right back to square one, to where you were before the desire arose. Another meaning of this is that desires once fulfilled do not end, but continue forming one after another. These desires multiply and never stop. That is why it is said that *Uma*, the virgin, is the energy of desire.

Observe the desires that arise again and again. Desire forever remains a virgin. The Ganga originated with a desire to meet the sea, but has this desire been fulfilled? If it was fulfilled, then why does the Ganga still flow today? Just as her flow is permanent, so is the power of desire. This is the meaning- the power of desire is *Uma*, the virgin woman. A virgin woman, or desire, can never meet the *Shivatattva* or *Atmatattva*, the essence of *Shiva* or the Self. One who attains happiness cannot have any desire. Is happiness possible when you have a desire?

"*Shivatattvamānanda*" – the essence of *Shiva* is joy. People often say, "When you remove the energy of desire, then you can see *Shiva*." That wish to remove the desire itself becomes a desire. When you say, "I want to eliminate desire," what happens? Desires do not need your permission to arise. Do they arise by themselves or do they request your permission to appear? You are hungry, and so there is a desire to eat, and when you are thirsty, there is a desire to drink.

Desires seem to arise automatically. When you struggle with a desire, how is it possible to relinquish the desire? You may feel that once you fulfill a desire, then you will be happy and contented, but this situation never happens. If you want contentment, then be content right now and do not wait until all your desires are fulfilled. People run after desires, constantly seeking contentment.

Knowledge of the self, or *yoga*, is knowing, "I am contentment. My nature is contentment." Who can give contentment to a contented person? Therefore desire is *Uma*, the virgin. The energy of desires gives you false confidence that it will bring contentment. It creates an illusion that it will lead you to contentment, but this is an fantasy. *Uma* remains a virgin, meditating upon *Shiva*. Have you seen the photo of Kanyakumari? It shows a beautiful young woman meditating on *Shiva* and holding a rosary.

Every desire meditates only on *Shiva*. Whatever desire you may have, what is the goal of that desire? It is to lead you to happiness. India lies between Kailash and Kanyakumari. Kailash means happiness. "*Kai*" and "*las*", where there is happiness and celebration. What is *vaikuntha*? The place where there is no scarcity. "*Kuntha*" means scarcity, and "*vai*" means absence, so the place without scarcity.

People visit Kailash and Man Sarovar as part of a pilgrimage, a *yatra*. Man Sarovar is the lake that represents the mind. Our ancestors honoured the mind so much. How is it possible to reach Kailash if the mind is a virgin woman, frozen and unmoving? The mind will find Kailash in itself when it becomes vast like a lake. It will attain the height that is devoid of scarcity and full of joy. So Kailash means happiness and Kanyakumari is desire. Desire gazes at the peak while in the south it meditates, suffering misery and pain, hoping to reach that goal.

People that say, "Cut off and throw away your desire," do not know what they are talking about. You cannot remove desire with this method. You can honour it and be a witness to it. The desire for renunciation or for liberation is also a desire. You may have rejected all the desires of this world, but then the desire for liberation arises. That desire is also *Shiva*. That same *Shiva* is meditated on by the virgin woman – "*Icchāśhaktir umā kumārī*."

Since ancient times in India we have been told to be useful to others and to wish wellbeing to all. After meditation, your consciousness is uplifted. During meditation, there may be no desires, but once you finish meditating, wish for everyone's wellbeing. You may fear desires, but when you have overcome fear, why would you desire petty gains? "*nānte sukhah asti yovai bhūmā tat sukhah*" – Let happiness be wide-spread and unlimited. Desire for this happiness and for the prosperity and well-being of all.

Even in the Jain tradition they say, "*mangalamkāmnah*" – desire for bliss or happiness. Buddhism proclaims, "*sarva mangalam*" – may all be happy; this is the desire they express. Both have the same meaning. All the religions of the world, including Hinduism, Islam and Christianity, have the same wish for everyone's happiness. Thus, desire continues, and we cannot say that this wish is the start or end of desire.

Desire is continual. It has no end, just like having food. You eat day in and day out. The desire of *prakriti,* of nature, never ends. If this were to happen, all of nature would come to a stand-still. The desire of nature existed in the past and is here now, just like waves of the sea, rising and falling.

If you stand on the beach at Kanyakumari, you can see the meeting place of two seas and an ocean. What do these three represent? They represent the three states- waking, dreaming and deep sleep. They also represent the three *gunas- sattva, rajas* and *tamas*. There are three types of desire- *sattvic* desires, *rajasic* desires and *tamasic* desires. The virgin Kanyakumari watches all three, remembering *Shiva*. In the world, all people are searching for *Shiva*; they are looking for that limitless, boundless happiness, which they are.

Do not think that a person will be completely happy once all desires are fulfilled. If all desires were to be fulfilled, he would become depressed. Depression is a problem more among the rich than among the poor. The poor have a desire for something more, and as long as they have that desire, they will not fall into depression. A person becomes depressed when his desire is fulfilled very quickly. Therefore, you find more mental illness in developed countries, where three out of ten children see a psychiatrist. Why do so many in the West become hippies? This is also due to depression. The faster desires become fulfilled, the faster misery comes. A person also becomes sad when his desire is unfulfilled, but one whose every desire gets fulfilled is in a worse state. So, when *Uma* Kumari, who has the energy of desire, which is a virgin, when she acquires the highest knowledge, then, "*ānandamvapule*" – the whole body fills with happiness. However, what happens to an ordinary person?

दृश्यं शरीरम्

Drisyam śharīram

"The body is scenery," or "Whatever is seen, all of that is the body."

This moment, you are seated and looking at me. So I am the object of sight, and you are the seer. When I am looking at you, you are the sight, and I am the seer. When you sit on the banks of the Ganga and look at the mountains, then you are the seer and the mountain is the seen. When you look, you think that the body is a part of you and that together you make up the seer. However, if your eyes are open, but your mind has gone elsewhere, you do not see anything. Why? This is because the mind is the real seer.

If the mind has gone elsewhere, the seer is also elsewhere, so how is it possible to see? How can a sight be seen? If the mind wanders, you may not hear all the words that reach your ears. Why? The mind is the listener. The mind sees through the eyes, but even with eyes wide open, you cannot see anything if the mind is elsewhere. Therefore, the real seer is not the body, but the mind.

This is the first step in inner progress: to stand outside the seen and be established in the seer. This is *yoga*. "*tadā dhruv svarupeavasthānah*" – to establish oneself in the form of the seer is *yoga*. Withdraw your focus from the seen, bring it to your vision and look at your body. Transform your body into the seen – "*drisyam śharīram.*"

Close your eyes and look at your body as scenery; this can be practical. What do we do when we do *yoga nidra*? We do the same thing. We lie down and bring our attention to each and every part of the body. We look at the body as the seen. This is the way to treat the body as the seen and the mind as the seer. Then the mind realises, "I am different from the body. I am a living, shining light." This experience happens. Everyone may have felt this in meditation. One meaning of this *sutra* is to see the body as an object of sight. This is a practice, a *sadhana*, which is directed towards this goal.

Sit and observe that you are the seer and your body the object of sight. If one identifies himself with the seen, he will be unhappy. A foolish man while watching a movie identifies himself with every character in the film. If the villain approaches the hero to beat him, the man watching the movie starts shouting. If the heroine starts crying, he also starts crying. Some throw stones at the screen, which even gets torn when enthusiastic fans of certain heroes and heroines throw tomatoes, eggs and so on at the screen. Generally, this happens in villages. Since the screen is torn, no further films can be screened. So the hero must win. Otherwise, if the person who the audience loves gets defeated the screen will be torn. This happened when M. G. Ramchandran acted in Tamil Nadu. People lost their minds by identifying with the characters. Their feelings went out of control.

Life is a mixture of intellect and feelings. You have to maintain the right balance. Normally, intellectual people sacrifice their feelings, and they resemble the living dead. They do not have even a bit of feeling in them though they may appear educated. They are dry and withered. They do not love and lack emotions and sensitivity.

On the contrary, sensitive people, who are full of love, cry at every step. Their mind never works, and emotions sweep them away. People in both categories wind up lonely. Fullness comes only when there is a balance between emotions and intellect.

The reason for misery is becoming one with the seen. If what is seen changes, then one also changes, and if something happens to the seen, the person is lost. The way out of misery is to detach oneself from the object of sight and establish oneself as the seer. If you consider your body as the seer, then you hurt when the body aches, and when the body feels pleasure, you feel happy. So the first step towards knowledge is to consider the body as the seen – "*drisyam śharīram.*"

Look at the body as you look at rivers and mountains. It is also beautiful and pure. Honour the body. Go further and honour the mind too. We have not only a physical body, but also a *manomaya,* mental body and a *sukhmay,* subtle body. The mind is also a body. Look at it. So many thoughts start and also end in the mind. The thoughts of the last ten years started there and ended there. You will realise your foolishness if you write down all your thoughts and read them after a while. The thoughts that arose twenty years ago vanished after five years. Not only did they vanish, but thoughts opposite to them developed. Thoughts go on changing. Waves of thoughts keep arising.

Never identify yourself with your thoughts. Witness them as though they do not belong to you. Thoughts change according to place and situation. They have their own dimension. Consider thoughts as the seen, and in a similar way, look at feelings as the seen. Who is the seer once everything else becomes the seen? You yourself will understand who the seer is. This is one meaning of the *sutra.*

"*Drisyam śharīram*" – the second meaning is that whatever you see, is your body. If the air is polluted, your body will perish. Is it possible to stay in a polluted atmosphere? If you are surrounded by poisonous gas, can the body survive? Therefore, even the air is your body. Similarly, the sun is also your body because without the sun, the Earth could not have been created. Your scope is not limited only to your body, but includes the Earth, sun and the whole creation.

Do you know the meaning of "*vishva*"? "*shva*" means past or future, and "*vishva*" means that which is without a past or a future. However, yesterday was there, and tomorrow will also be there. That means *vishva* will be forever. The meaning is- That which has not passed away or has not yet come, but which exists in the present moment, and so it is called "*vishva.*" If you are travelling by car from Rishikesh to Delhi, which is a six-hour journey. You can see the road clearly as you go. If you drive one kilometer, you can see that one kilometer of road. As you go farther, how far ahead can you see the road? When you look back, you can see only as far as your eyes let you. However, if you travel by helicopter, you can see the full stretch of road. You can see the road you have travelled and also the road you will travel; in other words, you can see the past, present and future in the moment.

Today we see light from the stars, but that light is not coming from the stars today. The light we see today may be as old as 4000 years. Therefore, "*vishva*" means without a past or a future, or in which everything is present in a special way. This *vishva* is your body. "*drisyam sharīram*" – whatever you see is your own body, is as good as seeing your body. Similarly, look around the world and consider nature as your own body.

You massage your body, decorate it and protect it. In the same way, look after nature because all of nature is your body. Look at a vegetable, which will become your body tomorrow. The food, which is in the market today, will be in your house tomorrow and will be eaten by you the next day. It all becomes your body. The world which was seen by you is your body now. So do not see any difference between your body and what you see. Or, look at your body as a witness.

हृदये चित्रसंघट्टाद् दृश्यस्वापदर्शनम्

Hridaye chittasanghattād drisyasvāpadarshnam

Merging the mind with the heart, objects appear with a sense of belonging to you.

Immerse the mind in the heart. Then you will always feel that what you see belongs to you. There are two ways to look at anything- one is with the heart and the second is with the intellect. If you look at the moon with the heart, it appears alive, but if you look at it scientifically, it is just soil and stone; it can be treated as a planet. Children only see the moon with the heart, and so to them, it is known as "*Chandamama*" – it becomes an uncle. A relationship is established. You may look at the River Ganga and say it is just flowing water, and others may see her as "Mother Ganga." We see her as a mother when we perceive her through our hearts. When seen with the intellect, material things are mere matter, and you cannot see life in them.

Soldiers receive specific instructions to look at enemies as mere objects, and not as human beings. If you look at enemies as human, your heart will take over and you will not be able to kill them. What you see belongs to you only when the mind is placed in the heart. What is happening today? People see the world through the mind instead of looking at it with the heart. Feelings dry out and then troubles start. We can recognise God in any object, animal or bird, provided we look with the heart. You will feel that they are also just like you. "*Hridaye chittasanghattād*"

Merging the mind with the heart is also a type of meditation. When we sleep, the mind merges with the heart. The moment we wake up, we feel a difference between heart and mind. In *bhavpūrṅa samādhi,* the feelings are awake, and the mind also is alert and awake. Other forms of meditation tell you to get rid of all your feelings and keep the mind as a witness. However, in this process you do not feel that all that is seen is actually you.

In India, people have always seen God everywhere. Even nature is considered a part of Divinity, and is called "*shrī.*" *Vishnu* has two wives, Shrī Bhūdevī, Mother Earth, and Shrī Devī, the goddess Lakshmī. *Vishnu*'s wife, *Shrī*, is *shakti*, or power. We treat the Himalayas and the ocean, called *Samudra rāja*, as kings. All the *purānas,* including *bhagavat,* describe them this way. We see the whole world as alive, not as inert matter.

Nature is not inert or dead. Why? This is because we see it with the heart. Just like children, we have looked at nature, merging the mind with the heart. Children see the sun, moon, trees, plants and even stones as alive. For them everything is alive. "*Hridaye chittasanghattād drisyasvāpadarshnam*" – whatever you see, you will see as belonging to you.

This is very important in today's world where friendship, feelings and compassion are missing between individuals. Positive qualities are lacking, and human values are ignored. This is a very simple *sutra*, teaching an important lesson.

The next *sutra* says:

शुद्धतत्वसंधनाद्वा पशुशक्ति

Shuddhatattva sandhānādvaa pashushaktih

When you are absorbed in purity, a sense of belongingness arises in you.

The principle of purity begins to emerge when you see that all are not different from you and all belong to you. Only when you feel that everything is part of you can there be purity and sacredness. "*apashu shaktih*" – it is not inhuman, animal energy, which is aggressive. "*Apashu*" means that which is non-violent, which accepts everything in itself and kindles the energy of love. This energy is stronger than aggression or physical force, and it is never violent or harmful.

In reality, children are the true masters of a household because anyone, whether he is a big industrialist or businessman, has to obey his children. Children rule the house because they have purity in them. They derive strength from purity. Purity is an energy of such high value.

Understand the difference between purity and impurity. Purity is to have a feeling of oneness with everything, and impurity is the absence of that feeling, a feeling of separation. When you mix water and oil, they do not blend – the water never feels that the oil is of its own nature, and the oil does not accept the water. This is impurity; such a mixture is called impure water or impure oil. Similarly, if sugar is mixed with sand, such a mixture is called impure sugar since sugar never considers sand as its own.

Water and milk mix well and become one. Sugar and water blend well; they have a good relationship. Sugar dissolves and becomes one with water. Water and lemon juice also blend well together. However, oil and water never go together. While nobody thinks a fruit juice is impure, a mixture of oil and water is called impure. When the natures of two things do not agree, then they do not bond and the result is treated as impure.

If we have that principle of purity, we feel a sense of belongingness with everyone. The feeling of separation disappears. You can unite with Divinity. You can meet God. When you experience this, *apaśu śakti* begins to shine in you. It is such a beautiful *sutra*, is it not? Such energy has no anger or aggression, and only with such energy is love expressed. In this world, there are many types of energy. Many energies are used for destruction, but *apashu shakti* unites.

Any vision depends mainly on the eyes. We perceive things according to the attitude of our mind. There is a saying, "Beauty lies in the eyes of the beholder." It is not in the object of sight. If the mind is pleasant, the whole world becomes pleasant, but if the mind and heart do not come together, it is impossible to be in a pleasant mood. "*Hridaye chittasanghattād drisyasvāpadarshnam*" – everything we see fills with life, and it stays alive.

From the point of view of science, everything is matter. From the point of view of spirituality, everything is alive. In the *Bhagavad Gītā, Krishna* proclaims, "The sun is a part of me; the whole nature is mine." If you want to feel this way, start looking with your heart, and not just through your eyes and intellect. Feelings are bright in the eyes of children, but when you look at intellectuals, you find no brilliance there – their eyes are not alive; you feel as though you are looking at a machine. When the ego disappears or when one is in meditation, you feel that everything belongs to you.

There are two types of energies: *pashū shakti* and *apashu shakti*. The first is a mechanical force, which has an aggressive tendency. The second one is alive. The energy of every animal, say an elephant or a buffalo, is limited – it is one-sided, filled with anger and lacking intelligence. *Apashu shakti* is alive and awakened. It is love. When you are absorbed in the principle of purity, *apashu shakti* starts to rise in you.

REST WITHIN

Weak people cannot experience wonder. We need strength in order to feel enthusiasm, joy and wonder in life. The body should be fit, and that is why the next *sutra* says:

स्वपदम्शक्तिः
Svapadam shaktih
You will find energy resting in yourself.

People work to gain strength. Whatever they do in life, they exert themselves only to gain strength, but they lose all their energy by working. Why do people amass wealth? They do it to acquire power and strength. Why do you want success and fame? It is because there is some power in that.

At home some children are quiet, and others will interrupt you when you talk with a guest. They say, "Mommy! I did this," "Daddy, I did that!" or "Brother! I did this," and show you the pictures they drew, or they bring their toys and arrange them in front of you while you are talking with your friend. Why do children do all this? This is to attract your attention. What do they gain by attracting your attention? They get power and strength.

Without strength, you cannot enjoy anything in life. When there is digestive fire, we want to eat. If you serve sweets or *vada* to a person who cannot digest them, he will not be able to enjoy them. A person who cannot open his eyes due to fever and whose body aches cannot enjoy beautiful scenery, even if you take him to see one. His eyelids would be heavy and he might fall asleep. Even if you took him to Heaven, he would sleep. What do you get from sleep? Strength. We lose energy chasing what we believe will give us strength. This would be clear even to a fool if he thoroughly analysed each and every instance.

Then, where is strength found? "*Svapadam shaktih*" – you will find strength when you rest in your Self. Instantly, strength will appear. You are strength! Your essence is strength – "*Svapadam shaktih.*" Whether others pay attention to you or ignore you, pay attention to yourself. You are paying attention to others; you would be better off if you turned your attention to yourself. You worry about what others think of you. Drop this attitude. If you turn your attention inwards, it will become a source of strength. Everywhere we struggle to find happiness, which is nothing but your own nature. You yourself are the strength you search for; you are a power-house of energy. In the Bible, there is a story:

A beggar dressed in rags went to see Abraham, the emperor. However, this beggar walked like a king. The gatekeeper stopped him and asked, "Where are you going?" to which he replied, "I have come to this pilgrims' rest house." The gatekeeper responded, "This is a palace, not a pilgrims' rest house." The beggar insisted, "No, take me to the king, the one who stays in this rest house." He did not listen to anyone, intent on being taken to the emperor.

Noticing his bearing, his manner of walking and the radiance of his face, the king bowed to him, as though compelled. Afraid, the king wondered who this man could be and questioned him, "Why did you say that you have come to a rest house? You have insulted my palace by turning it into a rest house for pilgrims." He answered, "I had come here before. Back then, another person was sitting here." "Yes, you do not lie. It is true that my father sat here." The man responded, "I came even before that time. Then too another person sat here." The king said, "Yes, I agree. What you say is correct. He was my grandfather," and the beggar replied, "Then what is this except a pilgrims' rest house? You sit here, believing that all this is yours. Many people have come and gone. Anybody who comes here stays only for some time. Is it not the same as a rest house? Nobody lives here forever. The whole earth is a pilgrims' resting house, where nobody has stayed forever. For this reason, I called this palace a pilgrims' rest house."

This knowledge struck the king like a lightning bolt. The moment he heard it, he descended from his throne and prostrated before the beggar. "You have opened my eyes! Take this resting house and look after it. I am going and leave it to you." Saying this, King Abraham left the palace.

You search for strength only after desiring it. The desire to be strong, makes people weak. The more ambition a person has, the weaker he becomes. Where there is a fear in the mind, there is no strength. If you have strength, there is no fear. Desire alone makes you weak. Nothing else can! Desire changes you into a beggar. Come back to your place, "*Svapadam shaktih*" – you become strength!

In life, we do not take total responsibility everywhere. What do we do? We take responsibility for particular things and not for others. If everything happens properly, we say "I did it," otherwise we blame someone else, saying, "He has done it." In a company there was a manager with two assistants. One was in the habit of complaining to his superior about mistakes committed by the people working under him. He blamed them when they neglected the work that had been given to them. The manager got tired of this blaming and started dealing directly with the workers, by-passing the assistant. What did the other assistant do? He assumed full responsibility for all mistakes. He would say, "I will look into the matter." The second assistant received a promotion. Many people suffer under the illusion that they will gain power by complaining or finding faults in others.

We have not found where our strength lies. We ourselves are strength – "*Svapadam shaktih.*" When you are strong, you can be innocent and loving. These are signs of power. Your mind should be childlike. "*Svapadam shaktih*" – know that you are in your place.

Look at a temple. A statue of *Vishnu* rests on top of the entrance gate and the same statue is in the inner sanctum. Have you seen this in temples? Make a round of the temple and you will find it. However, which one is worshipped? Position and place are important; they have value. So it says, "*Svapadam shaktih*"

वितर्क आत्मज्ञानम्

Vitarka ātmajñānam

Self-knowledge is possible through special logic.

You can reason anyway you like. Throughout your life you are involved in arguments and reasoning. This too is reasoning. Life does not exist without logic. Logic is necessary, but make sure that it is not wrong logic. There are three types of logic- *tarka*, logical understanding, *kutarka*, wrong logic and *vitarka*, special logic.

Wrong logic is finding fault everywhere; it is seeing a bad intention behind a good intention. Wrong logic tears you to pieces and disturbs your mind. Wrong logic brings misery.

Imagine that someone is irritated with you or someone else. Realising his mistake, he comes to you with sweets and other gifts to set things right. Then, *kutarka* starts in your mind: "Why has he brought all this?" or "Why is this person speaking so sweetly today. He must be planning something." Wrong logic is finding faults in all good actions.

Kutarka increases ignorance. For example, if you say the door is half closed, it also means the door is half open. If you say the door is fully closed, to conclude that the door is therefore fully open is wrong logic. This can never be the case. Although logically it might seem correct, practically it is false. In such arguments, you win only in words and not in reality. You might feel that you have won, but it is not so; you win the argument while losing the truth.

Due to wrong logic, pain, violence and trouble spread in society. We do not understand the difference between when we are using logic and when we have fallen into wrong logic. A sign of intelligence is to recognise the distinction between the two.

Logic is very important, but it changes constantly. Scientists found that the use of pesticides can produce good crops. They came to this conclusion through logic. Then another line of reasoning contrary to this logic surfaced. It said, "You feel that you get a good crop because of pesticides, but it has damaged the soil. The pesticides have ruined the soil's fertility and its mineral content. This has adversely affected the crops. Even if you claim that the crop is healthy, the people who eat it fall ill. Their health suffers from eating such crops." Once this argument started, the previous reasoning did not hold good.

The same is true of antibiotics. These days, people look to *Ayurvedic* medicines to protect their bodies rather than suffer from the side effects of allopathy treatments. They feel that the old methods are more reliable. The allopathy medicines you take to heal a stomach disorder have a side effect on the liver. If you fix the liver, the kidneys may be affected, and if you cure the kidneys, the heart may suffer. This is no treatment at all. You are merely moving from one disease to another, instead of treating the problem. Logic provokes, *kutarka* invites ignorance, while *vitarka*, increases knowledge.

Aurangzeb was very logical, but his reasoning used wrong logic. He locked his father behind bars and defended his actions with logic. His argument amazed everyone. He said, "My father is very old. He has lost his sight. He suffers and also troubles others. I am intelligent and can guarantee the welfare of all." He placed him behind bars in the palace and continued, "Now, what is required of him? I will ensure he is fed in prison. Let him rest. He is fine. Nobody needs to worry about him nor does he need to leave the palace to meet anyone." This was the tone of his argument.

Aurangzeb used to say, "Whatever could be written is contained in the Quran, so why do we need any other books? Therefore, all other books should be burnt. Collect all the books and burn them." This is *kutarka*. He is not the only example. You will find similar cases in your daily life and in every household.

You can build or destroy anything through reasoning. Generally, in school a subject is given for debate and the teacher asks the students to write in favor of and against the topic. Prizes are awarded based on how one argues, and not on whether one argues in favor of or against the topic. Sometimes people who have argued for and against a subject will both receive prizes. Argument is the only yardstick for the competition.

Logic has no loyalty. It can be used anywhere. The logic that pulls us down is *kutarka*. A person's downfall can happen due to *kutarka*. But the reasoning that can lift someone above argument to reach *ātmajñāna*, knowledge of the Self, is *vitarka*. *Vitarka* means special logic or thoughts without argument. Some people engage in logic and some others in wrong logic. Some are experts in wrong logic, and will twist their arguments to achieve their goals. Have you also done that at times? Observe the reasons you have given.

We had one devotee, a student, with us. He was told to do some work because he was young, and it was not appropriate to laze around. He would reply, "It is only lazy people who work. I am not lazy, but am doing *sadhana*." What did he mean by, "doing *sadhana*"? His argument was that lazy people work while intelligent people do *sadhana*. Who will counter this? People using wrong logic have their own dictionary to create their own words and to attach their own meaning to those words. Arguing only for one's own sake, even when a person knows that he is doing something wrong, is *kutarka*. Using such logic, we can never progress.

Knowledge can be acquired through analysis and logic. This is what science is. Analysis comes from logic. Knowledge of objects can be experienced, but knowledge of the Self is only possible through *vitarka*. If you want knowledge of the Self, then drop logic and apply yourself to *vitarka*, or special logic. This logic does not destroy anything. Spiritual knowledge and *vitarka* find unity in everything. It sees fullness and understands things as they are. Knowledge of the Self is an all-encompassing vision. It is the pinnacle of *vitarka*.

With *Vitarka* we create questions that have no answer. You can ask yourself, "Who am I?" This question is very complex. Merely asking this question will take you to such depth. *Vitarka* has no answer in words. You can know that a person is asleep from his snoring. If that same person gets up and tells you, "I am asleep," it will mean that he is not asleep.

Similarly, if someone asks you, "Have you seen God?" It will be better to be quiet. If you start speaking then "*Vichārambha vikāro nāmadhyeyah*" – words distort truth. You can understand only with the language of silence. The essence of the Self cannot be captured in words. "*Vitarka ātmajñānam*" – *vitarka* makes you introspective. If you keep asking, "Who am I?" all answers fall away and there is only silence. In the depth of that silence it is possible to have knowledge of the Self. It is certainly not possible through words. This is to be experienced; it is more important to experience it than to understand it.

One of the *sutras* says to move forward through love and feelings. Feelings and reasoning are opposite. There is no logic in feeling, and there are no feelings in logic. How many times is the same word used in songs? If you listen to music with the intellect, you might think that repeating words again and again is madness The mind questions, "What is the use of repeating the words so many times?" It is because there is love. The mind does not like repetition. That is why a person who is fully awake finds it difficult to listen to complaints. People do not complain once, but they complain over and over again due to lack of knowledge. Similarly, a person in love also repeats the same thing again and again. A rational person might not like this. He will become angry, and then boredom sets in.

Someone who is caught in logic cannot enjoy *bhajans*. They ask, "What is the point of repeating, 'Ram, Ram, Ram?'" The mind may have quite reasonably asked the question, but only someone who chants, "Ram, Ram," with *bhakti*, or devotion, will understand the effect of such repetition. If you repeat, "Ram" with devotion, then that power energises every cell of your body. You experience happiness and you start to go deep into your self. However, someone who looks at it logically will say, "I have said '*Om namah shivāya*' once. What is the use of repeating it?" Logic and feelings do not go together.

Laya samādhi happens because of feelings. What happens with logic? You can find *samādhi* with the mind's logic, but the logic should be *vitarka* and not *kutarka*. Then the mind will become peaceful. "Who am I?" is the start of *vitarka*. Throw away all the answers and hold on to the question "Who am I?" until you are enlightened. The only path to enlightenment is *vitarka*. That is why this *sutra*, "*Vitarka ātmajñānam*", has been given for those at a certain intellectual level.

Ganesha's vehicle is a rat. What does the rat mean? The rat is *vitarka*. It nibbles on everything in its path and cracks the covering of ignorance. That is why Ganesha sits on a rat. Neither Saint Kanakdas nor Shishunala Sharief studied in any university or college, but now university students write theses on their works. How did they get such knowledge? It came from *vitarka*.

If we look back on our life, we notice how time has flown by – 20, 30, 40 or 50 years have quickly passed. Everything in your life and everything around you has changed. You can understand this change. When you try to understand change, you may feel that there is one thing that has not changed, which draws your attention. You can feel the presence of the Self, which is unchanging, but you cannot see it. The phrase, "To see the Self or God" has no meaning. Can the Self appear in front of us as though a light has appeared and say, "I am *ātma,* the Self!" Did you see *ātma*? Who has seen it? Some people say they saw *ātma,* but that is not *ātma*. It is an illusion. *Ātma* can never be an object of sight. If you see your shadow, remember that it is not actually you, but your shadow.

Through *vitarka ātmajñānam*, knowledge of the Self, is possible. The moment this realisation happens, someone who was making himself more ignorant by logic will stop his arguments and look to *ātmajñāna*. Even if we receive only a flicker of light of *ātmajñāna* it is enough. "*Svātmānanda prakāsha vapushe*" – innocence, simplicity and joy enter life. They must come.

If one who knows the Self is unhappy, he does not really know of the Self. A person shouting on a street-corner cannot be a knower of the self, cannot be enlightened. He should have a cheerful mind! Joy should fill each and every atom of his body, just like a baby's. Look at a baby. How is it?

Suppose you did not get it; you did not realise self-knowledge. The next *sutra* continues:

लोकानन्दः समाधिसुखम्
Lokānandah samādhi sukham
The happiness of *samādhi* radiates waves of joy to the world.

"*Lokānandah samādhi sukham*" – this *sutra* is so full of meaning. It can be interpreted in many ways and seen from different points of view. Those who are realised and those who aim for realisation might have their own view.

From the point of view of the *siddha*, once you enjoy *samādhi*, the whole world is filled with happiness. When you are happy in *samādhi,* the happiness is not restricted to you, but spreads all around you. Something is wrong if you think that you are in *samādhi* while the people around you are unhappy. That cannot be *samādhi.* The sign of *samādhi* is that all should be happy.

You cannot hide light if it is shining. Its rays travel in all directions. If it does not spread, it is not light. If there is no happiness in the place around you, you cannot be in *samādhi* at all. Even if one person achieves *samādhi*, its effects radiate out to the world, creating happiness for people nearby. The effect when thousands of people enter *samādhi* can only be imagined.

When you pray, do not think that its impact is limited to you. Definitely, when you are peaceful, waves of peace spread around you and impact your surroundings. It has been said about Mahavir that anywhere within 20 miles of him, birds and animals would drop all violence. The waves radiating from him travelled far and wide.

"*Lokānandah samādhi sukham*" – is it possible that the happiness that overflows from you would not spread to all? If you have a cold, people who come near you might also catch cold. It is the same for coughs. If you stand near someone who is angry, you will become angry just like him for no apparent reason. Even if you are relaxed, you feel angry standing next to someone who is angry. If anger has that impact, why would happiness not have the same power? Is an impact of this type not there in *samādhi* or love? I tell you that their power is much greater!

"*Lokānandah samādhi sukham*" – when you are in *samādhi,* absorbed in meditation or in silence, rays of happiness radiate from you. When you see anger or rage on the face of a *sādhak,* who is trying to enter *samādhi*, it makes you ask what kind of *samādhi* it is that they are so unhappy. If there is fragrance, does it not spread?

"*Lokānandah samādhi sukham*" – from another point of view, you can say that everyone desires to be happy, and all the work they do is only to find happiness. Knowingly or unknowingly, people are searching only for happiness, which can only be found in *samādhi*. If you have experienced extreme happiness at any time, know that you were in *samādhi* at that moment. Do you know what happiness is? Where are you looking for happiness? Where is happiness to be found? What types of happiness are available to you in the world? Observe this.

You may really like a sweet that is made on a special occasion once a year. However, if you had to eat the same sweet morning, afternoon and evening, you would go out looking for spicy food instead. Looking at the sweet all the time would make you nauseous. Imagine that you went to a restaurant for a *masala dosa* or *vada*. If you invited the cook to join you, he would say, "No thank you," because he is so tired of smelling oil all day. He prefers rice and *rasam*. Since morning, he would have prepared hundreds of *dosas* and by noon has lost his appetite for them.

Any happiness you experience in the world comes with a tail called misery. Any type of happiness you experience in the world has its opposite. What is the use of water to someone who is not thirsty? However, one gulp of water will bring immense happiness to a person wandering under the hot sun with a dry throat. A person walking in the hot sun, when he finds a tree and rests under its shadow, will exclaim, "Oh, what shade!" The shade has a use when there is sunshine. If because of the clouds there is no sunshine, what will you do sitting in the shade under a tree? In such a situation, shade is everywhere. Without sunshine, you cannot enjoy the shade.

Similarly, to enjoy a meal one should be hungry. Likewise, with sleep- someone who is tired after a day of hard work will sleep well even if there are mosquitoes. Even rat bites will not disturb his sleep. But if you waste time during the day, then you will not be able to sleep at night even if you have a soft, comfortable bed. You toss and turn, and one mosquito's buzz will keep you awake. The mosquito is not responsible for your sleepless night. Your laziness will not let you sleep. If you lie in bed since morning, how can you sleep at night? People who oversleep cannot enjoy sleep, but those who work hard and tire themselves out in the fields find satisfaction when they go to bed.

In villages during festivals, especially during the Ganesha festival, loudspeakers continually blast music. People do not bother whether they play film songs or music – it may be a film song, Harikirtan, anything from Satya Harishchandra or Bhakta Markandeya. Some people do not see any distinction between them. Tired, the villagers sleep soundly despite the noise. Nothing disturbs them. The loud speaker goes on blaring. One person has been paid some fee, maybe fifty or sixty rupees, to keep changing the records on the gramophone. This happens even near our ashram. Those who come from cities do not get proper sleep, but the people who stay nearby sleep well. Once we had to send someone to stop the music man, saying "All your people are asleep now, so you can stop the music." He may need an extra ten or fifteen rupees to stop. You have to work hard to enjoy sleep. In this world, we can only enjoy opposite values in turn, but the happiness of *samādhi* is far greater.

"*Lokānandah samādhi sukham*" – the happiness experienced in *samādhi* is similar to, but greater than the pleasure and happiness we get in the world. There is no duality. There is no condition that you will enjoy food only when you are hungry. Anybody, whether elderly or young, rich or poor, educated or uneducated, can enjoy *samādhi* naturally. Such happiness is your nature. Once you have that enjoyment, then happiness appears everywhere. You are happy, because you are content your mind is fulfilled and satisfied whether you are looking at a garden or watching the sunset. You will not feel jealous even if you see others happy.

Suppose there is a group of four or five people talking, laughing and joking amongst themselves. An unhappy person suspects that these people are teasing him. If your mind is unhappy, when you see someone laughing, you will get indignant and scold them. The moment you blame a person or a situation, know that you are unhappy. Blaming others is a sign of our own discontent. When you abuse others, it comes from a weakness. Blame indicates weakness.

It is possible for those who have enjoyed *samādhi* to enjoy the world too. The whole world is full of joy. When someone offers a rose to us, we look at the thorn instead of the rose or we feel that the person has come to prick us with the thorn. We do not even notice the rose. Our nature has become like that. We must change this tendency. This change can happen only through *samādhi*. It is enough if even once you experience the happiness of *samādhi*, which is peace. Someone who drinks alcohol does not enjoy the taste of the initial two or three drinks. It is actually difficult until you start enjoying it. Whether it is alcohol, cigarettes or any other bad habit, the habit has to be formed. Then once it becomes a habit, you cannot escape it.

Similarly, get addicted to *samādhi*. The refreshing experience of *samādhi*, the cheerfulness it gives to the mind and its fragrance will impact your life. If you want happiness in this world in any work or in any field, it is a necessity to enjoy the happiness of *samādhi*. There will be duality in the world unless we experience the happiness of *samādhi.* Otherwise, we feel even pleasure as misery. There is no misery in life. It is we who create misery. It is in the mind. Misery exists in the mind which has not experienced *samādhi.*

"*Lokānandah samādhi sukham*" – this is a wonderful *sutra.* Imagine, you watch the sun set slowly in the west. You feel happy for perhaps a few moments, enjoying it. In those moments you have experienced *samādhi.* "*Lokānandah samādhi sukham*" – people search for happiness in various ways without realising that happiness is only found in *samādhi.* Every type of happiness is hidden in *samādhi.* "*Sarve padām hasti pade nimagnah*" – all other footprints are wiped away by the footprints of an elephant walking through the forest." Similarly, all other pleasures are trivial compared with the happiness of *samādhi.* That is why it is said, "Hold on to the happiness of *samādhi* and leave all other joys."

All other delights turn out to be bitter. Even if you enjoy *samādhi* for only a fraction of a moment, it will no longer matter whether or not you experience other pleasures. For example, in the morning when the sun shines, you do not say, "Light the lamp so I can see." Once the sun shines, it does not matter whether or not a small lamp is lit. Who would want the dim light of a small lamp with the sun shining?

"*Lokānandah samādhi sukham*" – once *samādhi* is attained, the happiness from it spreads. The whole world is searching for that happiness. This subject is discussed in the *sutra* very briefly. It is not necessary that all six billion people enter *samādhi,* but if even a few people walk the path of truth and if a few people enter into *samādhi*, the effect on others will be seen.

In the world, it is only a few people who cause problems, but all of society fears them. It is not that everyone is a terrorist. However, when only one, two, four or ten people become terrorists, they disturb the whole nation and alarm everyone. If there is that much strength in wrong-doing that they can terrorize everyone, then do you really think that goodness is weaker than wickedness? On the path of meditation, everyone gains happiness from it. Many undergo transformation. You can see its influence on people.

The happiness found in *samādhi* creates waves of pleasure in the world. If a person says he is in *samādhi* but he is unhappy and you can see it on his face, then something is certainly wrong. He has definitely not attained *samādhi*. The sign of *samādhi* is that waves of happiness spread in every direction.

शक्तिसन्धाने शरीरोत्पत्तिः
Shakti sandhāne sharīrotpattih
A body comes into being by the union of energies.

There are two subjects for inquiry. One is "I", and the other is "that". Science asks the question, "What is that?" while spirituality asks, "Who am I?" The body is created by the proper organisation and coordination of energies. Without the joining of two energies, the creation of a body is not possible, whether it is an ant's body or a human's. This is the only way to create a body. This is natural and clear. Whenever a body is created, there is a union of two energies. Understand this energy. Observe it. Then you will understand the knowledge of a body's origin.

These days, cloning is being done everywhere. Cloning is not a new subject. In India, Gandhari did it. She made 100 pieces out of an embryo, and placed them in 100 pots and heated them. However, who was born out of this – Duryodhana, Dushasan and others – is another matter. Gandhari made it possible though. What were they if they were not test-tube babies? History would not describe cloning unless there was some truth in it.

It is said in *Rāmayāna* that Ram flew back to Ayodhya in an aircraft. They must have had a vehicle that was something like an aircraft or else why would that word have been in use or even created? Something like *pushpak vīmāna* may have been there. The people then certainly had an understanding of these things.

"Shakti sandhāne sharīrotpattih" – this *sutra* only mentions that by the fusion of two energies a body is created. After it is created, the life and spirit enter the body. "*Chaitanyodaya*" is another word for this. This *sutra* explains how consciousness is brought forth in something. In Himanchal Pradesh, the statues of gods shake, tremble, dance and write. Scientists do not understand how the statues move. They have been filled with *Chaitanyodaya*. Consciousness has been brought forth in them. This is a very deep science. The statues made from bronze, stone or *panchadhātu*, a mixture of five metals, move and write! This is very difficult to understand. You may have read or heard about it. The energy of *prāna* is moving in them. If you go to Kulu or Manali there are many such figures there. Consciousness has been invited through *prāna vidyā*, which causes consciousness to enter into the statues. *"Shakti sandhāne sharīrotpattih"* – from the union of two energies, the body is created.

This *sutra* also means that both the energies are equal. It is not that either man or woman is superior. Both energies are equal, and only through their union can bodies be created.

भूतसंधानभूतपृथक्त्वविश्वसंघट्टा

Bhūtasandhāna bhūtaprithaktva vishvasanghattāh

This world is created by the union and separation of the five elements.

This world is created by the union and separation of matter in the form of the five elements. If you look at water, when you divide water you get oxygen and hydrogen, and from these two you can produce so many other combinations. If five elements are split up, many new combinations can be produced. In the same way, an atom can be split into two, releasing tremendous energy, which is eventually used to generate electricity.

In the same way, this world is created from the five elements – water, fire, air, earth and space – and the world moves due to the union and separation of these five. This *sutra* is the start of science. If you mix the elements in different ways, you get different things! The existence of the world is based on their coming together and then separating. "*Vishvasanghattāh*" – this is not merely a belief, but it is a science. When at first a principle or rule is given, which you then try to understand, you are starting with belief. Science works differently; in science, subjects are understood first and then accepted. The world's religions ask that you first accept and then understand. Science says, first understand and only then accept. You cannot say, "I understand it, but do not accept it." *Shiva Sutras* can be read from both angles. In India, science and religion were never in conflict. The religious and scientific subjects of India are not only for belief, but they are scientific truths. You can understand them, study them and experience them yourself. It has also been said not to accept anything without first-hand experience.

Birth and death are both the same – they happen because of the coming together and separation of five elements. We have called these two processes birth and death. The body is made up of millions of cells, and when all these cells decide not to stay together but to separate, the body starts coming apart. Love engulfs each and every atom in creation. The principle that holds everything together is love, and the same principle also separates everything.

When you observe the sea from an airplane, you do not see the rising waves. You see the ocean, but the waves and bubbles look still – you do not see the movement of the water. Only when you are near the sea do you notice that new waves are continually rising. You do not think that it is one wave, but groups of waves appearing again and again. It is an optical illusion. Similarly, the play of the five elements makes it appear that this creation exists and has no creator. It is not that someone created all this and then left it and is sitting somewhere far away. When you come close, you can see a river's flow, but if you look at it from another angle, a river is part of a cycle that includes river, sea, clouds and again the river. All these are one cycle. However, when you look from the normal point of view, everything looks static.

When you see a fan turning, it looks like a spinning plate. You do not see the blades. This creation and its ways are like this. Let's look at it from another angle- suppose creation is not created by any individual and that the waves rise and fall on their own. It is the sea's nature. That is why Jain philosophers said, "God is not sitting somewhere. All actions happen according to a principle that is called '*karma*.'" Guru Nanak called this "*hukam*," or "*ājñā*." Everything happens because of *ājñā, karma*.

If, after creating this whole creation, God left it, then he cannot exist everywhere. But it is not possible to keep God away from what is, wherever it is. It is like a pot and clay – a pot is made from clay, but now is different from the clay. However, it is not possible to see a pot without the clay. The clay has become the pot.

In the same way, this world has come from God, and it is God. Therefore God is present in each atom of this creation just as clay is present in the pot. Creation has been created out of five elements in addition to consciousness. Therefore God is called "*upādāna karma*", the cause. That is to say, the clay has become the pot. There is no potter who prepared the pot. If the potter or God had a different existence then God would not be present everywhere. Nobody has created waves in the ocean, but it is the ocean water that has become the waves. Did anyone come to create waves? It is impossible. The waves have started by themselves. Similarly, the creation out of five elements has taken place by itself. The Creator is not different from the five elements, and he is not sitting somewhere else having created the elements. God is interwoven in this creation. Science accepts the truth that this creation has been created by God. It only searches for how it was created.

शुद्धविद्योद्याच्चक्रेशत्वसिद्धिः

Shuddha vidyodayāchchakre shatvasiddhih

When pure knowledge dawns in you, everything belongs to you.

When pure knowledge dawns in you, impurities and the feeling of "others" vanish. The moment you come in contact with pure knowledge, everything in this flowing cycle of existence belongs to you. Everything in creation is cyclic.

Only a confused person is unhappy while only a person who has a clear mind can be happy. *"Svātmānanda prakāsha vapushe"* – this is a sign of intelligence. Know that if a person is unhappy, then he is not really intelligent, though he may think he is. Unhappiness is born from a lack of intelligence.

When intelligence vanishes, anger comes. When we do not have a broad-vision, intelligence is lost. Where there is greed, the intellect stops working, and intelligence at that point becomes narrow and limited. When you look at the world with broad vision the intellect has no use. Intelligence understands: "From where did this world come?" "From where did I come?" "What am I made of?"

The difference between people and animals is that in people, intelligence has blossomed, while in animals it has not. Then "*satya shuddhih*" – the intellect is purified. Let us understand the distinction between pure and impure intelligence. Impure intelligence looks at the present from the point of view of the past. It holds on to past experiences and looks at present experiences with those old spectacles. The inability to understand the present as it is, is called impure intelligence.

Pure intelligence sees the present as it is. It helps to distinguish between logic, wrong logic and special logic. Such vision is an expansion of pure knowledge. Pure intelligence looks at truth as it is without being swayed by emotions. If you look at a situation or person emotionally, you do not see the situation as it. You only impose your own views and emotions on it. When you look at a situation while you are stuck in your feelings, you say, "Oh, I feel so and so about this situation." How to escape this trap?

Everyone says that, what he sees is true, which depends on his own personal experience. Nobody is ready to see situations as they are. People tend to cling to just one way of thinking, claiming that only their way is correct while other ways are all wrong. There is so much of ego. How do we know whether our knowledge is wrong or right? Look at the truth from different angles. When you see it from various points of view, then you have a broad perspective. Thorough knowledge investigates a situation from different angles. For example, you have impure knowledge, if your wife complains about your mother you get angry at your mother and quarrel with her based on your wife's complaints. Similarly, if your mother complains about your wife, you believe her and shout at your wife. This situation results from impure knowledge. What does a person do who has pure knowledge? He will very patiently listen to both points of view and just keep quiet! Do not entertain such complaints, which are short-lived. Their complaints are an outpour of bad feelings towards each other, which were present in their minds. Anyway, what was to happen between them has happened. Patiently listen to them and keep quiet. A similar thing happens between brothers and sisters. Even mothers have the same problem with their children. Look at each situation with pure knowledge and see the problems simply fade away.

GURU IS THE WAY

The mind is just like a *mantra*. We can realise this if we examine the mind and the intellect. When a thought arises in the mind, it is not easy to get rid of it. The thought keeps coming back over and over again, and if you decide to do something else, you will feel uneasy until you finish with that thought. It becomes irritating like a grain of sand in the eye. Observe the state of the mind in this situation.

If someone gives you ten compliments and one insult, what does the mind hold onto? It clings to the one insult. It comes to the mind again and again throughout the morning, afternoon, evening and night. Similarly, if you are unhappy about something, that sadness does not easily leave you, whatever you do to get rid of it. Even by listening to inspiring discourses that sadness does not go away. "*Lokānandah samādhi sukham*" – everything is full of happiness, but where is it? The mind discards good things and clings to misery. Many times you tell your mind that something is trivial and not to worry about it. What happens after you tell your mind this? The mind or intellect does not pay any attention. So what do we do? We chant a *mantra*. What is the use of chanting a *mantra*? Our mind takes the form of the *mantra* that we repeat.

A person's face and nature become like the one that he worships or thinks about over and over again. That is why we say, "Look at his face." Since we cannot see the mind, we look at the face. Many times, the face reflects the mind. If you look at the face of a person who is always scheming, you immediately know his intentions and you become alert. Similarly, look at the eyes of someone who is greedy – they look at others as though they will gobble them up. Greed streams through their eyes. Miserliness can also be seen easily, and anger can be seen in the face of an angry person. For them, becoming angry is a habit, like a *mantra*. If you get angry again and again in the morning and evening, anger becomes a *mantra* for you. Look at a person who worries – you can see it in the dullness written in bold all over his face. He sits there as if the world had fallen on his head. They give off such vibrations. If you keep worrying, you will have worries following one after another.

Mullah Nasruddin always complained, from morning till night. If coffee was served, he would say, "My wife has given me too much coffee." If coffee was not served, he would complain that it had not been served. Sometimes he complained, "There is too much sugar in the coffee," and at other times, "There is not enough sugar." In a year when there was plenty of rain, and the crop was good, some people thought that there would be nothing to complain about. Then Mullah said, "Everything was fine, but because of too much crop there is more workload. I am not used to so much work, and now I have to harvest this." He never stopped complaining.

The mind of a person who habitually complains has made complaining his *mantra*. In order to be happy and pleasant, we have to practice being full of joy – *ānandamayojyās*.

You may have observed that some children, despite falling and getting cut, are happy and smiling. Other children cry even before falling because they are afraid of falling. One can cry after falling, but to start crying before anything happens is not normal. The feelings in our mind keep repeating themselves. Often, people who worry too much feel compelled to visit astrologers and temples. If you look at the faces of the people who visit temples, they are all worries and anxiety. They think they will feel relief after receiving blessings at the temple, but in reality, they are not sure.

To keep the mind happy, one has to form a habit. How to be happy? One way is by chanting a *mantra*. "*Manah trāyate iti mantrah*" – means a *mantra* is that which is brought to mind again and again. How to practice this? The mind and the *mantra* should not be separate. The mind should become the *mantra*. For this, you can use any *mantra*.

What happens to us? We want to follow a *mantra*, but the mind goes elsewhere. We chant, "*om namah shivāya, om namah shivāya,*" but inside we wonder whether or not our son has left the house or what is cooking. All such thoughts occur while people chant *mantras*.

If the mind thinks of something else while chanting the *mantra*, the *mantra* will not be effective. The mind should be filled with the *mantra*. The moment that happens, the mind is free from worry. What is worry? A worry is something that is not in place.

It is neither here nor there. A *mantra* is necessary to drive out worries. What is there in a *mantra*? A *mantra* has strength and spirit. When these are present, the mind becomes the power of the *mantra*. The power of the mind and the power of a *mantra* are the same. For example, when we sing *bhajans* or chant "*Shiva, Shiva*," the mantra becomes powerful, and the mind becomes filled with consciousness. When consciousness increases, we come back to the *sutra*: "*svātmānanda prakāsha vapuse*."

चित्तं मंत्रः
Chittam mantrah
Mind should become the *mantra*.

"*Chittam mantrah*" – it means this is how the mind should be maintained; the mind should be prepared this way. This is also a great experiment. Observe the mind carefully. The tendency of the mind is to return to unwanted thoughts. So much energy is drained from the body every time we think. Every thought is equal to 1000 volts of electricity – that much energy leaves our system. We are using two wrong *mantras*, which we need to remove from our mind. One is that we brood on misery over and over again, and the second is that we keep calling back anger. This is called *ārdra* and *roudra*. The mind gets disturbed and the body weak because of *ārdra* or *roudra*, and then the body falls ill. Use a *mantra* in order to rid the mind of these disturbances. How to use a *mantra*? The mind should be immersed in the *mantra*. The mind should become the *mantra*.

The mind is always engaged in something. It is always touching, tasting, listening, etc. You may smell some fragrance at the beginning of meditation or at the end you may see lights. All of this happens either at the beginning or at the end. But meditation is different from all of these experiences. "*Dhyānam nirvidya manah*" – meditation is the absence of sense experience.

This is a subtle way to quiet the mind. *Mantra japa*, repetition of the *mantra*, should start after meditation. If you are meditating with a cheerful mind, you can experience the vibration and the power of *mantras*. This is called *mantraviryānubhava*. The power of every *mantra* can be felt in the form of vibrations.

When an atom explodes, its impact spreads not only for many kilometers, but the effects remain for many years – all this from the explosion of an atom! The mind is a thousand times subtler than an atom. Imagine the power of the mind when it becomes quiet. When the mind becomes quiet again and again, this is called *mantra*. *Mantra* is the cure for the mind. Whether the *mantra* is "*Om namah shivāya*" or "*Rāma, Rāma*," the effect of the *mantra* depends on how it is pronounced and invoked.

When a *mantra* is read out of a book, it has no value, but when it is chanted in *satsang* or after receiving it from a *Guru* it is alive. For example, "*Sohum, Sohum*" can be read by everyone in a book – it is written everywhere – but only when it is said in a particular way can its power be felt.

Once, a *Guru* had a disciple, who requested the *Guru* to give him a *mantra*. At an auspicious time, the *Guru* gave him the *mantra*, "*Rām, Rām*." The disciple was disappointed and unhappy. He had known this *mantra* since a long time and wondered whether it had really been necessary to undergo so much hardship just to get this *mantra*. He approached the *Guru* and said, "You gave me

Rām mantra! Give me something new. Show me a miracle. My grandparents also repeat '*Rām Rām*.' Everyone chants '*Rām Rām*.' What is so great in it? Teach me some other *mantra*."

Then the *Guru* gave him a small stone and told him to go to several people and find out the value of the stone. The disciple was told not to part with the stone, but only to find out about its value. So he went to the market, approached a vegetable vendor and asked him the value of the stone. The vendor took the stone in hand, and said, "This is a beautiful stone. I can use it as a weight. I will pay you ten rupees. Give the stone to me." As his guru had told him not to give the stone away to anyone, he did not give it. He noted, "The vegetable vendor is prepared to pay ten rupees." Then he went to another person and asked about the price. He offered to pay one hundred rupees for the stone. After asking many others, the disciple went to a dealer in precious stones, who offered one lakh rupees, saying, "This stone is beautiful and rare. Please sell it to me." Now the disciple became troubled and afraid. He was confused why from morning to evening some people were willing to pay handsomely for the stone, some were only willing to pay ten rupees and then there was a trader who was ready to pledge his life and serve the *Guru* for ten years in order to get the stone. The disciple did not understand all of this.

The disciple told the story to his *Guru*, and by that time his mind had changed. He understood that the *Guru* had transferred the fruits of his *tapas*, his penance, to the stone. Only those people that had sharp minds and were aware were able to grasp the value of the stone. Although a *mantra* may be the same, its value is different when given by a *Guru*. Then you feel the power of the *mantra*. When the *mantra*, "*Om namah shivāya*," is chanted in *satsang*, have you felt the vibrations of the *mantra*? When you come in contact with that *mahātattva*, that greatness, when your mind is at peace, you can experience the real power of the *mantra*.

Some people go to temple, constantly chant *mantras* and chime the bells non-stop. However, they do not experience anything because their mind is not meditative and there is no spirit or feeling behind the chanting. Each and every word becomes a *mantra* if it is full of meaning and feeling. A *mantra* is not only a word with some meaning. It contains a feeling, and when we go beyond the feeling then we experience the strength and power of the *mantra*.

"*Yo jāgātham sacakkājyam yo jāgārtham sāmānyanta*" – the *Vedas* will run after those people who have a meditative state of mind. They will easily understand the *Vedas*. Guru Nanak said, "Knowledge of the *Vedas* and other spiritual knowledge come not just by reading books, but naturally flow to those who follow God and act according to his wishes." The *Vedas* sing the song of divine consciousness.

"*Chittam mantrah*" – there will not be any difference between mind and the *mantra*. Both become one. You can control the mind by using a *mantra*. With the help of a *mantra*, the mind loses its smallness and becomes vast; the mind that is dissatisfied becomes content; and the mind that is constantly disturbed by desires is released from them and finds fulfillment.

Desires keep on arising in the mind. Desires, yearnings and animosity have overtaken the mind. Some people's minds are entirely filled with hatred. Their minds are like oases of hatred.

Some people's minds are only angry. You can see anger in their eyes, face and ears. Anger oozes out of their body. If you look at the faces of some people, you can see a mind full of worry. They look as if the sky has fallen on their heads. Such a state of mind leads to misery. A mind in this state cannot swim, and it drowns.

One method to find a solution to overcome the mind is *mantra*. "*Chittam mantrah*" – there will be no difference between mind and *mantra*. All the behaviour and tendencies of the mind are in your consciousness, just as the essence of a tree is in the seed. Then what is a seed? It is a full tree in itself. Similarly, what is a *mantra*? A *mantra* is also a full tree. The energy of life is in the *mantra*. In it, you can find the seed of your goal. Through this seed, life's aim is attainable. The tree is the ultimate aim, but what is its root? Its root is the seed, in which the tree can already be seen. Similarly, with the help of a *mantra* the mind reaches its goal at the end of life.

प्रयत्नः साधकः
Prayatnah sādhakah

This *sutra* tells us to put in our full effort. Our mind does not wish to hold on to the high road. We become lazy. One learns *pranayama*, but there is too much laziness to actually practice. Many times, those people who have learnt, practice, but the teachers do not. They teach *yoga* to everyone else, but they themselves do not practice. This should not be the case – "*Prayatnah sādhakah.*"

Some people ask, "Do I have to meditate twice a day? Is it not enough to meditate once a day?" If they are told to come to the course and meditate, the immediate question is "How many times a day?" And if they are asked to come for four to five days, they will ask, "Is four days enough? I cannot come the fifth day." If we agree to four days, they will ask, "Is it OK if I come only for three days?" If they are told to come for one day, they will come only for an hour, or they will make an excuse like, "My mother-in-law is coming from Mysore so I have to go to the railway station to pick her up." The point is where your priorities lie.

It is stupid to think that there is no time. This is only an excuse: "I don't have time," or "Who has the time?" Whether you ask a bank employee or a labourer, "Do you have time?" his reply is- "Where is the time? I work from morning to evening and no sooner do I come home than I fall asleep." Nobody, right from the prime minister to a labourer, has spare time. Yet they do different work. How is it possible that some people are able to accomplish so much? It is only an excuse to say that there is no time. Why? It is to hide laziness. We say there is no time and blame work. We have to get rid of laziness. We will be happy only when we drive out laziness. The misery that bothers you is due to your laziness. That is why we have to put in effort.

"*Prayatnah sādhakah*" – distance yourself from laziness. We cannot even describe how far our laziness extends. We are lazy with everything. We keep the light switch near the bed near the bed so we can turn it off while in bed. Tea is served while you are still in bed. As conveniences increase, diseases also increase. Observe a person who has worked hard. He enjoys a good rest, while those who do not work hard are unable to sleep, but toss and turn in their bed. One who is on the path, a *sādhak*, should put in good efforts. Make these efforts a *sadhana*.

If less than our full effort is put in, the mind gets bored and frustrated; it will feel some lack. We should put in full effort to get rid of this lack – we should put in 100 percent effort. Then the mind becomes quiet.

We need to be a little awake to judge whether our efforts have been made to the full extent possible. Rest and sleep can wait till after death! While we still breathe, let us not waste our time sleeping in bed. Put in effort. Put in 100 percent effort. That is why it says, "*Prayatnah sādhakah.*"

If a *sādhak* feels that he and his efforts are separate then he gets tired, and if he gets tired working, there is a possibility that he will quit his efforts. If he works for someone else, he will get even more tired. But when he works enthusiastically for himself, he will not get tired. When your son or daughter's wedding draws near, you are busy with preparations. You work day in and day out, but still you are not tired, but you cannot even work for half an hour for someone else. If you had to do eight hours of work, you can only imagine what would happen. When you are forced to work for others or do not want to work, you get tired after just three hours.

If you are putting in effort, and there is a difference between you and the effort, then you become tired. *Prayatnah sādhakah* is true only when life itself becomes an effort. This seems to be the reverse of what was said before. In the beginning it said to drop your efforts. Now it says, "Do any work and get involved in it so much that you do not feel tired." "*Prayatnah sādhakah*" – that is *sadhana.*

When the mind is in agreement with any work that we do, whatever it may be, we do not feel tired or find pain or misery in it. It does not matter whether you succeed or fail in that work. You will be free – that is certain. It hardly even matters if you make a profit or loss, because the work is a pleasure. While operating, a doctor puts in his 100 percent effort for the patient. Whether the patient survives or dies, the doctor feels relieved for having put in his best effort. If the doctor puts in effort only to ensure that the patient survives, but he does not make it, the doctor will be sad. It is not possible to save all patients. If the doctor has not put in 100 percent effort, his mind will be upset, whereas if the doctor has put in his full efforts he will not feel regret – "*Prayatnah sādhakah*"

गुरुरुपायः
Gururupāyah
Guru is the means.

People who approach a *Guru* and ask, "Please show me the way," do not have any common sense. It is enough just to consider the *Guru* as your *Guru*. Anyone with innocence and an open mind automatically gets the energy of the *Guru*. Sometimes people feel dull before they come to *satsang*, but as soon as they come and sit in the *satsang*, consciousness starts flowing through them, and they feel alert, energetic and enthusiastic. This is a sign of a *Guru*. *Guru* is the means. Once you accept someone as your *Guru*, in time you will be able to see the nature of the *Guru* in yourself.

That much devotion to your *Guru* is enough. Kanakdas did not attend any university, but he still wrote many poems. He had the necessary faith and devotion. His *Guru* told him, "Go, 'buffalo' is your *mantra*." He started repeating, "Buffalo," and a buffalo came to him. This is not only a story. There is some truth to it.

Nobody has seen God, and it is difficult to believe in a God who you have not seen. The *Guru* is visible to us, and in him we can see trust, love, peace, naturalness and strength. A relationship can be made with a *Guru* that you can see. "*Gururupāyah*" – *Guru* is the means! If you cannot make an effort, at least come with an open mind. In putting in effort, your ego grows, and you feel, "I am doing something."

So far, two *sutras* have been given, which are very important. One is "*prayatnah sādhakah*" – put in your best effort, and the second one is "*Gururupāyah.*" You come to a guru only after you put in your full effort, but still feel defeated. Then you do as the *Guru* advises. It is very difficult to find a *Guru* in this world. One meets a *Guru* because at some point he has done some good work. There are very few who take advantage of a *Guru* even if they meet one. After using all the means, you have faced defeat in life, and *Guru* is the last means. When *Guru* becomes the means, then there is no defeat in life. Your perspective in life shifts. So it says, "*Guru* is the means."

शरीरं हविः
Sharīram havih
The body is an offering.

Once you have approached a *Guru*, blaming yourself is out of the question. There is no room for it. If there were room for blame, then it would be as though you had not come to the *Guru*. What is the meaning of approaching a *Guru*? It is not just walking up close to him, but to have that trust and faith that the *Guru* is with us, that he will provide whatever we need, he will guide us and our life will flow smoothly. Such a deep faith will develop on its own.

We need to remember one thing. "*Sharīram havih*" – our body is pure. "*Havih*" is the offering we put in a *yajña* or *homa*, the sacrificial fire. A *yajña* is happening in this world, and your body is just an offering. Your body is offered in the flames of time. Time is moving just like you are moving. In front of our eyes, 20, 30, 40 years have passed. Yet you have not woken up. There is no time for knowing where you are. Life is coming to an end, and the body has become an offering. Look with honour at this passing life. Offer it as it is. Do not cling to it. For this to happen, you need a feeling of surrender.

We offer our body at night, but take it back in the morning. That is how people surrender. Someone told me, "Each day as I go to sleep, I surrender my body and the next morning I take it back as I have more work to do." But this is not how it is. When we make an offering into fire, once it enters the fire it becomes ash; the result can be seen. The offering cannot return as it was. This is the nature of fire. Similarly, once your life starts it burns in the passage of time, and cannot remain the same. If it stays the same, then you are inert and not human. People undergo transformation. In a song, Akka Mahadevi sang, "You do not accept offerings from those who do not transform." Life is an offering. This body is an offering. So with this attitude, offer it up and wake up to life. Then there will be no possibility of worrying, and we will come back to life. Then, "*Svātmānanda prakāśā vapuse.*"

ज्ञानमन्नम्
Jñānamannam
Knowledge is food.

As your body requires food and sleep, in the same way your soul requires knowledge and understanding. The root of all problems- worry, hatred and misery is lack of knowledge. If you have knowledge, then there is no misery. Where there is misery, there is no knowledge. Understand this. When your stomach is full, you do not feel hungry. If you feel hungry, then your stomach is not full.

Look at the faces of some so-called wise people. Their faces are full of worry and misery. If they are wise or knowledgeable, they should be cheerful and full of happiness. That is why it says, "*Jñānamannam.*"

If you are unhappy, then you need knowledge. Go into some knowledge and examine your life. Try to analyse it. Where are you heading in your life? Many times you have been born, cried and died. Now wake up and look around. Life is a celebration, in which you grow in knowledge and celebrate life. Knowledge is "*Sharīram havih*" and "*jñānamannam*" Knowledge is food for you. If you have knowledge, your pleasantness and enthusiasm will increase and overflow. The more you know, the more your mind will be full of happiness. Misery is not your nature. Do not think that misery is inside of you and go searching for it. Sit quietly and think about the words of knowledge that you have listened to, and your mind will become happy.

Why do you attend *satsang*? Although you may not understand all that has been said, whatever you have heard washes impurities away from you, and the mind feels relieved and happy. Otherwise, do you know what happens? Half-there, you listen without paying attention or you nod off. That is why many philosophers and wise men have come to this world and given discourses, but most people are still sleeping. At any point in time, it does not look like anybody is awake.

FROM DARKNESS TO LIGHT

Every time a fire-cracker is lit, it creates a loud sound, bringing your mind and consciousness into the present moment. That is why we use fire-crackers. It is like shock therapy. Without the noise from the bursting fire-crackers, the mind does not come into the present. The mind is constantly dreaming and wandering elsewhere. Observe the mind's fantasies. We have no time to study them, though dreams constantly come up.

विद्यासंहारे तदुत्थस्वपनदर्शनम्
Vidyām samhāre taduttha svapnadarśanam
When knowledge is lost, dreams start.

In the previous *sutras* we looked at "*Gururupāyah,*" "*Sharīram havih*" and "*Jñānamannam.*" This *sutra* is a continuation of those *sutras*. You are continually day-dreaming. This fire-cracker is only there to wake you from your dreams. Every *sutra* is a fire-cracker. It should bring light to darkness. Do you know why we celebrate *Diwali,* the festival of lights? The month of Karthik has the longest nights of the whole year. It is the month of darkness. In this darkness we need to light lamps. There is no point lighting a lamp where there is light everywhere. Darkness is not unnatural. Many dark moments come in life, and people keep sleeping in the darkness. That is why we celebrate this festival, in which we burst fire-crackers to wake up.

Living in society, among people, sometimes hatred and anger arise. Some disturbance or argument takes place with those with whom we do not have a good rapport. All the differences of opinion we have are not with enemies, but only with friends. We store all this anger and hatred in some corner of our mind. Let it all come out at once and be sent away. This is the reason for bursting fire-crackers.

Normally we do in the outside world whatever is happening inside us and vice versa. Whatever happens inside is reflected outside. When you are in a good mood, you give someone flowers, but if the mind is disturbed, then you stare at him or you pick up a rock. There is a relationship between our mind and our behaviour, and our behaviour also gets reflected in the mind. People always mix up one with the other. That is why the mind is happy when you burst fire-crackers, light candles or arrange flowers for offering. *Diwali* is celebrated to kindle a light inside you that will never die.

Why are we in such a state when our nature is light? Why are we not happy? That is why it says, "*Vidyām samhāre taduttha svapnadarśanam.*" "*Vidyā samhāre*" means loss or destruction of knowledge. Knowledge is lost, so dreams arise. It means that somewhere inside, the link with knowledge has been broken. What are you dreaming about? There are three types of dreams.

Dreams of success- we think, "Everyone must garland and clap for me. Everyone should appreciate me." The cause of the mind's dreams is the desire for praise, and no amount of praise is enough!

Mullah Nasruddin was honoured in some country by someone. Once the program started, Mullah eagerly looked around to see who was present at the event. Somebody asked him, "Why are you upset today? Why do you not look happy? What's the matter?" Mullah replied, "I have been given so many garlands, but I cannot see anyone from my village in the crowd. It would have been fine if I was not honoured. I am unhappy because I was honoured, but nobody from my village witnessed the event." We desire that our own people praise us.

In every house the husband is pleased if the wife praises him. Sometimes, though the whole village praises him, his wife will scold him the moment he walks in the door. His own wife does not praise him! It is the same with the wife. While others may praise her, she will only be satisfied if at home her husband praises her! She is unhappy if someone comes home and praises her while her husband is out of the house. There is eagerness that her husband should hear the praise being showered on her by others. She thinks, "If only he had heard!" Suppose that somebody compliments her in the presence of her husband then she looks at him, as if to say, "What do you think of me? See, you do not praise me. Do you know who I am? Now at least do not say, 'the shrubs in the garden are not of any value.'" We carry on this way in all situations. While sitting, we dream of praise.

Dreams start small and grow big. It starts with wanting to be famous in one's village, then in your country and then in the whole world. One desires that all the daily and weekly papers should publish one's photo and name. Those in the film industry want recognition. After gaining recognition, they are afraid that someone else will reach the same height of fame; they want only themselves to be at that level, and that the fame they have gained must not be lost. They want to hold onto that status. This is another great problem- everyone wants to everyone else to think that there is nobody like him. It would be difficult if there were somebody else like him!

Someone went to Rishikesh, met a great *sadhu,* a holy man, and told him, "I have not seen anyone who has renounced more than you have. The *swamis* of other *mathas* enlist more and more disciples in order to be called '*Guru*,' but look at you – you have no disciples or anybody with you. You are truly detached." The *sadhu* was very happy. He said, "Yes, what you said is true. All others build institutions and live there. I am a real *sadhu*, a truly great soul." The visitor said, "Yes, you are a real *rishi*. In Uttarkashi I saw another *rishi* like you. You at least keep a water-pot and wear clothes. That *sadhu* does not have even those. He wears only a loin-cloth." The *sadhu* was crest-fallen because of pride. Arrogance is a lack of knowledge. The moment knowledge is lost, arrogance starts to grow. What is a sign of arrogance? "*svapnadarśanam*" – continual dreaming that this or that should happen.

The second dream is for money- I should have bucketfuls of money. How much is not at question, but it should be lots of money. How much do you need? One lakh? Two lakhs? One million? Two or three million? Lots of money – there is no end to "lots of money." "Lots" is a word for lawyers. Someone might file a case against God, saying, "I asked for lots of money, but you have given me less." This "lots of money" is one of the reasons for our unhappiness. The mind that is not full wants more. When the mind is full, it is contented.

The other preoccupation is for authority. What is this desire for authority? Only the weak, who lack strength, want authority. A strong person does not desire authority, but instead desires to serve. Understand this fundamental difference. Those that feel that strength comes from a group or crowd are weak. Weak people are ambitious to get authority, and they fear that very thing for which they are ambitious. A weak person is afraid that someone will shout at him. Those in a union are weak. They fear those in authority. They start union activity because alone they have no strength. To show power they shout in a group. No individual is responsible when shouting in a group. A group is never responsible. If any work is done in a group, a person can say, "I did not do it. Someone else did it," or, "I did it, not he." Saying this, they try to escape. All weak individuals join together to form a group.

A strong person deals with criticism patiently and with an even mind. Nobody can rob him of his happiness or contentment. If someone becomes mayor or chief minister, he will not be content until he becomes prime minister. It is difficult to meet any chief minister in a state capital, but you can meet anyone in Delhi because they are all there. There is lust for power – they dream about it. Only when this lust for power is released can there be happiness.

Thirdly, we dream about sense pleasures. Why do some people have many affairs, even after marriage? They think they would be happier with another man or they would be better off with a different type of woman. There is no contentment. That is why kings of the past used to have several wives. Even today some people from Arab countries marry several times.

In our country, no task is more difficult than searching for brides and bridegrooms. In spite of this, people keep thinking about marriage. They wonder whether it would have been better if they had accepted an earlier marriage proposal. Even on the day of marriage, they keep thinking, "Was this the right or wrong decision? I have tied the *mangal sutra* on the bride. Am I caught in a bondage now? I had only one chance in life, and now it is finished." At that time they are very unhappy. That is the reason a band is tied around the bridegroom's head. It means: let the mind be where it is instead of dreaming of something else. The headgear symbolises keeping the mind under control. The headgear is put on the forehead because the minds of men are more unsteady when it comes to marriage, whereas women accept what comes as a blessing and stay quiet. So to keep the wavering mind steady and under control, men wear this headgear.

"*Vidyām samhāre taduttha svapnadarshanam*" – every moment we are moving towards the grave. One day, this body will be soil or ash, and that will be the end. Remembering this brings knowledge. "*Jñānamannam*" – whenever the food of knowledge decreases, dreams increase. In dreams, you are either in yesterday or tomorrow. Live in the present moment. When we bring our mind into the present, we are full of happiness. We see ourselves as joy and happiness. When this happens, there is no distance between you and God. Your own nature is bliss. The more you are in the present, to that extent you are one with God; to that extent you are established in the self; to that extent you are pure consciousness. Then life is enjoyable, and you return to the first sutra: *"Svātmānanda prakāśā vapuse."*

On white cloth, dirt stands out. People wear coloured clothes to hide dirt. A bed will be covered with a coloured bed-sheet. Whether it is white or coloured, the cloth gets dirty. But dirt cannot be seen on coloured cloth, whereas it is clearly seen on white sheets. Similarly, small matters in our mind appear big.

Even a speck of dust that enters the eye can cause so much pain and irritation, while a pile of mud on the head will not bother us so much. That means that one can ignore a big worry, but cannot tolerate a slight botheration. The mind is like that. It is so sensitive that it gets disturbed even by an insignificant remark. And when the mind is upset, the surroundings affect it more strongly.

If you go to a place where there was a fight earlier, the moment you arrive you feel tense. When this happens, a *sādhak* gets frightened. He starts thinking, "What happened? I meditate and listen to knowledge. How did I get angry?" He starts to blame himself.

Some years ago, a 72 year old *swami*, a seeker and a pious man, visited our ashram. The ashram's atmosphere is uplifting – the mind becomes happy and it does not wander elsewhere. One day somebody invited the *swami* for a meal in Bangalore, so he went and came back to the ashram. The next day he said, "I was so disturbed I did not sleep the whole night. I started to have sexual urges. Why did this happen at this age?" That such an elderly *swami* told this so openly speaks a lot about his honesty. Afterwards, he himself analysed the situation and explained that this was the effect of the food he had eaten. His mind returned to normal the next day.

When one's mind is cheerful, one cannot tolerate greed, jealousy, attachment, lust and anger. When you are happy and suddenly you see someone and become jealous of him, that is unbearable for you, is it not? Then you blame your own mind. Our downfall starts the moment we start blaming ourselves. Why? Then we become ready to blame others. At first, we blame ourselves, saying, "My mind is not in order." Then we say, "Others are wrong. He is no good. That person is no good." We start finding fault with others and hatred begins. Self-hatred brings hatred for others, and with this, your years of *sadhana* will have been in vain. Your cheerful mind will be spoilt. Everything will be finished.

PLAY OF THE DIVINE

आत्मा चित्तम्
Ātma chittam

Your mind is your self.

"*Ātma chittam*" – your mind is your self. Do not leave your mind in search of the Divine. This mind also belongs to God, and the disturbances in the mind are also a play of the Divine. We should treat them as a play or entertainment.

If you read any old *purāna*, or ancient story, you find only anger and jealousy. Lakshmi got angry with Sarasvati. It was a fight between mother-in-law and daughter-in-law! Sarasvati is the daughter-in-law of Lakshmi. That is how we trap the Gods in the anger and hatred that is in us. All the *purānas* contain anger and hatred – whatever happens on earth also happens in heaven. Chandra stole the wife of Guru, also known as Brihaspati. A fight ensued between Guru and Chandra. "Chandra" in Sanskrit means the mind, and "Guru" knowledge. Knowledge says one thing, and the mind says something else. That is why everyone knows that smoking is a bad habit, but people cannot stop.

This *sutra* says something very important: "*Ātma chittam*" – day, night, clouds and colours all appear in the sky and later disappear. Similarly the mind imagines many things, which disappear just as they came. You may have gotten angry many times, but do you stay angry forever? Just as light fades away in the evening, anger also fades away. It is the same with envy. There is a limit to everything. When one thought rises, another falls away. Where does it go? All is in our mind. That mind is the Self. Clouds may cover the sky, but the purity of the sky remains untouched. Whatever may be the state of mind, the Self is pure. There is no such thing as a bad Self. As anger is a quality of the Divine, it is also a quality of the Self! That is why it is said, "*Ātma chittam*" – the mind itself is the Self. The mind is part of the Divine.

When we say, "Do your *sadhana*," it means *sadhana* needs to be done daily. This is because there are millions of cells in our brain. Some work today, and others work tomorrow just like workers take shifts in a factory. The factory is running continually, but the workers have shifts – they come, work and leave. Similarly, in our brain, neurons work in shifts.

We can only say Jayanagar is educated when everyone there has received an education. There are millions of neurons in your brain. For them to gain knowledge, all the neurons need to be trained. When we are educating the neurons we say, "*Om namah shivāya,*" over and over again. Some neurons are trained today, others will get trained tomorrow and others will be trained the day after tomorrow.

Through this process, one day you will reach perfection, *siddhi*. Do you understand? This will happen only if *japa*, repeated chanting, or meditation is regularly done. That is why this is emphasised. If you skip a day, then those cells that are on duty that day will not be trained. They will have to wait for their next turn, and until then, they sit there untrained. That is why we daily practice is necessary.

"*Ātma chittam*" – everything is of the very nature of the Self. This is a very valuable *sutra*, and when we understand it, it leads to discrimination and knowledge.

कलादीनां तत्वानामविवेकोमाया

Kālādīnām tattvānām aviveko māyā

When we see a situation in a limited way, the knowledge obtained will also be limited, and we feel, "My life is only this."

Do you know why we have astrology, or *jyotisa?* Do you know the meaning of *jyotisa?* When you face problems, if you look at the problem from a broader angle, you say, "Oh! I am under the influence of Saturn." When we recognise this, we accept that a situation happened according to our fate and do not blame others. We simply think that someone made such a comment because of fate. It means to look at any situation with broad vision and not with narrow vision. In the Kannada language, we say, "My *grahachar*", or "My fate." It is a very valuable phrase. We pass over an incident saying it was because of fate. The aim of astrology is to find a reason for why ideas arise in the mind and situations happen. It could be that they happen because of the movement of certain planets. To remove the negativity, some methods may be given, such as to do meditation or *japa*. There are millions of cells in your brain. Educate all of them.

We say *purusha* – "*puru*" means town and "*purusha*" means the one who lives in town. *Purusha* does not only mean man, but includes women also! Similarly, our body is also a town. Do you know how many worms and bacteria live in your body? The intestine alone has more than 50,000 types of bacteria, which number in the millions. There itself they have water and electricity supply. They experience an earthquake when we eat spicy food. What for you is dysentery is a flood for them. They have established their own towns inside you. We do not know about it. Similarly, the incidents that happen in consciousness can be known only through the principles of *kalaa akaala*.

Many elements are produced in our body – elements of fire, air, water and so forth. One element starts in our body and the other in the environment. If the fire element arises in a place where everybody is quiet and happy then a fight breaks out. A wise person understands this well before it happens. In advance, they realise, "They are all going to fight." With some interest, you can also get this knowledge. Similarly when the air element stirs up, all the people who are sitting down feel an urge to get up and go. Even while sitting, they fidget with their legs and hands. Some people tap their hands in the office, even though the person sitting in front of them is writing carefully. They are not aware of others. They sit and move their feet around without thinking about time or place. Such people have excess *vayu*, air element.

Similarly, when *pitta*, the fire element increases, you think too much. Suppose someone is late by a half hour, worries start about what accident has happened. All unwanted, useless thoughts start. You decide not to think this way, but again you start thinking the same way. Why is it so? This is lack of discrimination. Such anxiety is born out of lack of discrimination and lack of knowledge.

"Kālādīnām tattvānām aviveko māyā" – This is called *māyā*. In any situation, know that the faraway stars and planets are responsible for it and also that I am responsible for it. Either take responsibility or blame it on the stars. Either way, you will not blame anyone or fight with anyone.

Another aspect is waiting for the right time to come. There is an advantage and disadvantage to this. Thinking that a better time will come, you stop putting in effort, and this brings laziness. By misusing this science, we have killed astrology. We do not understand its inner meaning. There are two groups of people. The first type blindly believes whatever the astrologer says while the second type does not try to understand anything about astrology and brushes it all off as a bunch of lies. Very few people try to understand the truth of it. For this reason the science is losing recognition.

"*Kālādīnām tattvānām aviveko māyā*" – means to see things in a different way. The interaction of many factors causes something to happen. An incident happens because of effort, a favourable environment, grace, patience and time. Suppose you want to sow a seed. For that you have to choose the right time to sow seeds. What happens if you sow when everyone else is harvesting? Whose mistake is it? The factor of time has not been accounted for. What if the seeds were sown at the right time, but not watered? Then a mistake has happened. Lack of discrimination set in, and full effort was not given.

The world is not simple. Creation is a great secret and very complicated. It is a little difficult to grasp. Creation is mysterious, and nothing in it is straight-forward. We need to understand this clearly.

Do not hold any person responsible for an event. There are many factors involved – the state of his mind, circumstances and so forth. To understand all of this is "*Kālādīnām tattvānām aviveko māyā*"

Because of *māyā*, a person does not know that he is the Self. We think of *māyā* only as money. Some are very happy hoarding money – they go on collecting and storing it. I knew one elderly lady, who had collected one hundred rupees in coins. She would keep all the coins in a box and count them from one to a hundred every night. Her mind was contented, feeling that she has lots of money.

Similarly, there was a wealthy businessman, who had turned the money which he had accumulated into gold bricks, gold ornaments, gold coins and so on, and they were all hidden in his basement. Every night before sleeping he would go downstairs, look at all the gold and sleep happily, knowing that he had so much wealth in the house. Every night he did this. The day of his death drew closer, and all the children had gathered there. Now this man was a miser and though he accumulated money, he did not spend it nor did he let others spend it. His son came and asked him, "Father, how is it that you go to sleep so happily?" He knew what the reason for his father's happiness was, but wanted to confess something to his father before he passed on, so he said, "I have to tell you something. The gold you think you have is nothing but brass! I have sold the gold and replaced it with brass! You were feeling happy every night looking at false coins!" The father felt as though a bolt of lightning had struck him, and he died a day earlier than expected.

We used to read *Chandamama*, a children's magazine. One story went like this- there was a king whose life was in a parrot, which was in a cage. The cage was in a fortress, which was far away beyond seven seas and then seven mountains. Only if the parrot's neck was chopped off would the king die. Similarly, we have placed our Self, our life somewhere else. Some people keep it in gaining a nomination for the election. If they lose the nomination, they feel like they will die. Some place their life in their children. If daughter or son rebels or if the daughter-in-law moves out of the house with the son, they lose their will to live. We do not keep our life with ourselves. Often, we keep moving it from one place to another. At first, it may be in toys, then later in neighbours, children, grandchildren, lottery tickets or some other similar place.

We live as though we are marching in a funeral procession to take the dead to the graveyard. That is why we do not see the spark of consciousness in people's faces – because our life is not with us. Kabir has said, "This is a town of dying people. Why are you living here? This is a town of dead people. Here people are dying every moment. All the dead are here."

"*Atma chittam*" – your mind is the Self. You are of the nature of Divinity. You do not have to go to temples, churches or mosques and ring the bells. Wherever you are, be there with a contented mind. Rest in your mind. Understand the mind's mischief. You are the Self. Your body and the atmosphere are made up of the Divine. Anger, hatred, jealousy and other negative qualities that appear are also made up of the Divine. Understand "*Atma chittam.*" Not understanding this is lack of discrimination, *māyā*. Keep in mind that in reality, all this is happening in the mind.

LIBERATION FROM LUST

This one mind of ours sees through the eyes, hears through the ears and tastes through the tongue. The same mind feels experiences in each and every part of the body – hands, legs and other limbs. Who is experiencing all these sensations through the five senses? One mind experiences the world in five different ways, through the five doorways of the senses. From this arose the five elements, which can be experienced on the physical level. Similarly, the mind thinks with the intellect and stores impressions in memory. Ego is- "I should do this or that," or "I should be like this or like that." This is how its ideas get expressed. Like this, the whole world is made up of twenty-four elements or principles. Some say it is twenty-four, and others say sixteen. The counts are different in the various *shastrās*. But all of these elements continue acting by themselves.

The energy of an atom is the same everywhere, but the same atom is different in coal than it is in diamond. You can make *idlis* and *dosas* with rice. With the same rice, various dishes are made. We also make noodles, cooked rice and lemon rice. These are prepared separately, and so we do not mix them, but eat them separately.

Similarly, this world, though it started from a single principle, has different forms with different functions. Not understanding this is *māyā*. If you look from the perspective of this one principle, then you find that principle everywhere.

What is our body? It is a bag of blood, bones, flesh, nerves, and a brain – a sack of many elements. It is a machine, which has the ability to think. Yet this is not how we look at people. We do not say, "See how many sacks are here," or when a guest comes, "Look, a thinking machine has come."

People think that *māyā* means money. Even this has some meaning. It is not that it is without meaning. Why do we need money? We need money to protect this body, to have clothes, to maintain a house to live in, to go here and there and in order to do work. Money is required for everything except breathing. It is required for us, for our happiness. Yet there is no point holding onto money just to have money.

Once, a very wealthy businessman was ill, and as his last days came near, his relatives all gathered around. The doctor asked him, "What is your final wish?" The businessman was very sad. When everyone expressed their sympathy, he said, "I am not crying because I am dying. I am not concerned about that. What should I do with all the wealth that I have earned? My children are useless, and I do not want to give it to them, nor do I want to give it to anybody else. That is why I am worried. After working my whole life, I have amassed so much wealth. What should I do? I do not want to die, leaving my wealth." He could not take the wealth with him after he died.

Somebody suggested he consult an astrologer to find out where he would be born in his next life. The astrologer said that he will be born in a particular house near Tumkur in Shira Talak and that he will have such and such name. The businessman was very pleased. He called his lawyer and had a will made out, leaving all his property in that person's name. The businessman said, "Now I can die in peace! I have nothing to worry about. I am going to recover all my property. I have not wasted this life. It has been fruitful." The person was content that he could enjoy in the next life what he had earned in this life. This is attachment.

Māyā is ignorance of the elements, or principles. Knowledge is understanding that everything in our body is changing. We are unable to have knowledge because of attachment. There are two causes for creation in this world- attachment and lust.

Without lust, there is no creation. Lust is present in every animal, bird, creature, plant, tree and human. You were born because of lust. It is the start of creation. That is why *Devi* is called "Kāmākshi" and "Kāmeshvarī." The whole world is full of *kāmakoti*. What is meant by *kāmakoti pītha*? This world has not only one lust, but millions of particles of lust are there. Desire is filled with the creative power of creation. *Shakti*, or energy, sits on the seat of desire. But nobody sees this energy because lust blinds us. The awakened consciousness does not stay with us. It becomes the flame of desire. Everyday creation happens because of lust, and it is nourished by delusion. Do not look down on lust.

We scorn desire. The only culture that does not look down on desire is the ancient Vedic culture. That is why we worship the *linga*, and not just the *linga* but the *linga* and the *yoni*. The highest worship is honouring the *linga* and *yoni*. We also worship *Manmatha*, calling him the Lord of Desire, *Kāmadeva*, and celebrate the festival of desire. What we worship does not bind us. Usually, we cling to what provokes us. Suppose you fight with your spouse, neighbour, daughter-in-law or mother-in-law. Your mind will think about them even when you visit a temple, and on your way to the temple your mind will be scolding them. God will not be on your mind even though you worship and chant his name. Our mind is far from the object we worship. This is an important psychological path- our mind will be free from whatever it adores, up till the very point when devotion fully blossoms. We are in bondage to whatever we look down on. The people who keep on condemning desire really have desires inside, but they blame it on the world.

Many of us do not know Sanskrit well. If you read any of the 108 or 1008 names in praise of the Divine – the *Lalita Sahasranāma* or *Vishnu Sahasranāma* – and read the names of the Divine written there, you will feel like closing your ears after hearing the gross descriptions of the various body parts – huge buttocks, hefty thighs, large breasts, the goddess with breasts like an elephant's head. Why were these descriptions used? Had the *rishis* lost their minds that they would think like this? Were their minds so sick? These questions come up. Only those who are daring and have clear, pure minds can say such things.

You may have a *Vrataratna mālā*. If you open it, you will see that it contains praises of each and every limb. In any *vrata*, or observance, whether of Ganapati, Vāra Lakshmī, or Svarna Gauri, the practice is to worship every limb of that form of the Divine.

Worshipping in this way, the mind, which is attracted to a particular body part, is liberated from that obsession and becomes peaceful. That is why when we worship *Vishnu*, we start from the feet and rise to the head, worshipping every part. This is a great secret of adoration of the form of the Divine. Through this practice, we can gain victory over desire.

If you want to gain anything or rise above it, this can only happen by honouring that object. Only with reverence can you rise higher in life. *Hanuman* worshipped *Rama* and by doing so became greater than *Rama*. Ravana fought with *Rama* and went down defeated. *Hanuman* knew fourteen arts, while *Rama* only knew twelve. *Rama* could not have accomplished anything without *Hanuman* by his side. There is a story that *Parashurama* fought with *Rama* and though he lost, *Rama* bowed to him and called him *bhārgava*. *Rama* won! Likewise, *Hanuman*, a devotee of *Rama*, offered himself to *Rama*. One who surrenders with reverence rises higher and becomes more powerful than the one he honours.

So creation happened out of lust and is maintained by attachment.

मोहावरणात्सिद्धिः
Mohāvaranāt siddhih
Perfection happens through a veil of attachment.

This is such an amazing *sutra*, the likes of which is not found anywhere else in the world. You cannot put a value on this *sutra*. *Siddhi*, perfection, happens because of a veil of attachment. People abuse desire. Attachment is also abused. It is true that we should not hold on to attachment and that it brings misery. The same attachment though, brings protection.

When a dog or cat gives birth, it protects its own offspring. How is this protection possible without attachment? Does a dog leave its pups and go elsewhere? A sparrow brings food and feeds its newly hatched chicks even if it does not have enough food for itself. The sparrow cares for its young because of attachment. Similarly, a tree spreads it seeds with full protection and care. If a coconut dropped from tree without the protection of the outer husk, it would crack. But the coconut is made so that it falls with the husk, which is so light that it can float. So the water carries it away and deposits it somewhere on a bank where it sprouts and becomes a tree. That is how the tree spreads its seed. Cotton seeds go out with the cotton, as though the plant says, "Fly in the wind." Similarly, animals protect their young. Wherever a cat goes, it carries its kitten by holding its neck in its mouth. Have you seen a cow that gives an angry glare to anyone that troubles its calf? It is only through attachment and the feeling that "this is my offspring, and I must raise it and protect it" that the young receive care.

To do any work in the world requires some attachment. In foreign countries, there is no attachment within the family, and that is why there is no family there. There is desire, but without attachment behind it. This is known as prostitution- where there is no permanence in the relationship. A relationship needs some attachment in order to be permanent. Children will not be cared for unless there is attachment for them. If the attachment is not there, the relationship will not last. The main problem in the West is that there is no bonding in the family, and so there is no happiness. Whether attachment is too much or not at all, it creates a problem, like having too much salt or not enough salt in food.

"*Mohāvaranāt siddhih*" – attachment to knowledge is what brings you to listen to knowledge. Some people ask, "What is the use of *bhajans* and *satsangs*?" You will not reach perfection with an attitude of indifference, saying, "Let's give it a shot. Something might happen." You will not find fulfillment this way.

Only when you feel attachment towards music can you learn to play an instrument, whether it is the *veena*, the *taboori* or the *tabla*. If you are learning how to use a computer, you will perfect your skills to the extent that you are attached to the computer. But where there is a half-hearted attitude or something is done just to pass time, learning will not be complete. If you do not feel attachment for a pastime, your efforts will not be successful.

Even to pass an examination, you need attachment for the subject. If you are studying *Ayurveda*, then be attached to *Ayurveda*. Perfection comes only to the extent of your attachment to that field.

Some obstacles may be there. On the way to achieve success, difficulties will crop up. See it as a test. Some have few problems and others have more. Yet the more attachment we develop, problems bother us less. We do not even look at them as problems.

Even very poor people living in huts and under tin roofs by the road side have such attachment toward their children.

A *swami* went and stayed as a guest in an elderly gentleman's home in Kanpur. Since the son and his wife both worked outside the home, this elderly man did all the household chores like sweeping and looking after the children. When the son returned home in the evening, he would scold his father, and once even slapped him in front of the *swami*. The *swami* felt pity for the elderly man and asked him, "Why do you struggle so much? I feel badly for you. Come stay at my ashram where I'll look after you and you'll live comfortably. At this age, after having lived 70 years, why do you stay with your son who abuses you? Why lead such a life? Please, come."

The old man, who until this point had been pouring out his sorrows, suddenly became enraged and said to the *swami*, "Did you not have any other home to break apart? Why did you come only to my house? Go; find some other house to ruin. If I leave the house, what will happen to the children? What will happen to the grandchildren? My son and daughter-in-law work outside of the house. Who will feed the grandchildren? Who will sweep and clean the house? Please, do not ruin this house. Leave." Shocked, the *swami* wondered, "What is this?" Out of compassion I offered him a place to stay, feeling that he is such an elderly man who struggles so hard. I didn't want him to live in such conditions and offered him a better life, but he turned against me!"

This is attachment. Even after being kicked around, you stay somewhere because of attachment. Even if it means dying, you stay there. There are some who refuse to leave their old house and move to a new home. They say, "Even if I die, I will not leave this place or this village." Such attachment for a place and for people! If attachment stays within limits, it will bring success. But if the same attachment exceeds its limits, it brings misery. So it is said in the next *sutra*:

मोहजयाद्नन्ताभोगात्सहजविद्याजयः
Mohājayādanantabhogāt sahajavidyā jayah

With victory over attachment, you find unlimited enjoyment, naturalness automatically arises in you, and you can succeed in any work.

There is no use getting entangled in the abilities and successes you gain after winning over attachment. So you achieved some success – say you became an expert *veena* player. If you hold onto the thought that nobody plays the *veena* better than I do, your ego gets bigger, and when you meet someone who plays the *veena* better than you, jealousy starts. Your calm poise and cheerfulness vanish. When you see someone close to you talk with someone else and smile at him, your stomach churns because you feel that he should speak only to you and to no one else.

A newly-wed couple keeps a close eye on each other just like a good watch-dog guards the house. They observe whether the other is looking at someone else or not. The way they keep an eye on each other, even dogs do not keep such close watch! What do they keep an eye on? If one smiles at someone else, the other suspects he is thinking about that person. They wonder whether their mind is being distracted, and they try to bind each others' mind. You cannot even control your own mind! Why do you try to control the mind of others?

"Mohājayādanantabhogāt" – When you win victory over attachment, you find unlimited enjoyment. The satisfaction that we feel when you accomplish something through attachment is very little. *"Mohājayādanantabhogāt"* – your happiness and your

consciousness are unlimited. To enjoy such vast happiness, you need to escape from attachment; let go of small pleasures. If you do not rise above attachment, the small mind will only think, "What about me…my son, my daughter, my mind." Just as your children belong to you, your neighbours' children also belong to you. "Everyone belongs to me" – you can win over attachment only when this feeling dawns in you. Many times you have heard people advising detachment. Everyone, even *sadhus*, recommend finding freedom from attachment.

Many people become *sannyasi*- renunciates, out of fear of attachment. They leave everything and run away, imagining that they can escape attachment. Although they leave home, they become attached to their possessions – their water-pot, saffron robes, images of devotion, *danda* stick, etc. If someone touches or takes their staff, they get upset and shout. Then they become angry and hurl abuses at others. People tremble in fear of *Gurus* because of their harsh words. It's commonly said, "One should feel fear and devotion for an elder." Either you are afraid of him or you have devotion for him. There can be either light or darkness. Just as light and darkness cannot be present together, fear and devotion cannot exist together. How can there be fear when there is devotion? We say "fear and devotion" only as a figure of speech.

"Mohāvaraāt siddhih" – to find greater happiness and unlimited enjoyment, you need to rise above small pleasures. If you drown in them, there is no use. The happiness or achievement you get out of attachment is limited, and what is limited comes with a tail; that tail is unhappiness. You cannot make anything with only pure gold. You have to mix it with some other material in order

to make jewelry and ornaments. Similarly, a small amount of unhappiness is mixed in with all your happiness. But if you win over attachment, you can have unlimited pleasure and the endless experience of the Self.

Krishna was named Mohan. What does his name *Manamohana Giridhadhārī* mean? "*Manamohana*" means the one who attracts the mind and can bind it completely. This is needed for a married person. Keep on increasing your attachment and move ahead. Let attachment happen toward your unbounded Self, consciousness. Be attached to greater happiness, and do not be satisfied with small things. This is contradictory. Sometimes we say to be satisfied and at other times we say not to be satisfied. Both should happen at the same time, not in sequence. Both satisfaction and dissatisfaction should happen together. This is very subtle. "*Mohana*" means the energy that attracts things to itself. This divine energy, the energy of knowledge, the energy of the *Guru* is known as "*mohana*". This attraction is so powerful that in comparison every other happiness seems small.

The happiness you feel in *satsang*, the joy of devotion, once you experience this spirit of devotion, you will not find joy in anything else. When, in complete surrender, you dance or sing, forgetting yourself, endless happiness, joy and bliss can be felt, and compared with this joy, all other pleasures seem small and tasteless.

"*Sahaja vidyājayah*" – when this happens, you will be natural. Naturalness will arise in you on its own. It means you do not have to put in any effort. You can do any work as easily as drinking from a glass of water. When this happens, your mental faculties grow stronger, and any work you do at that time will be successful. Good results will come naturally and quickly.

Some people spend five to ten years learning how to fix a television. Those with *Sahaja vidyājayah*, though they may not know anything but they push a few buttons here and there and the television starts working. It is similar with car repair. Many people get a mechanical engineering degree, and then to repair a car they simply go through a manual, and with a few screw drivers some time are able to fix a car by doing one thing or another. What do some drivers do? Although they may not know anything about a vehicle, if the car stops, they pull some wires here and there, and the car is fixed. A mechanic knows about a vehicle very well and can do the work easily. Similarly, those with *Sahaja vidyājayah* can easily achieve success in all their work, and life becomes smooth. They are able to face any difficulty with a smile, peacefully, and move ahead.

जाग्रद्द्वितीयकरः
Jāgrad dvitīyakarah
The waking state is like our left hand.

"*Jāgrad dvitīyakarah*" – this means the waking state is like our left hand. It is as easily and readily available as water. We think that the waking state is something great, but it is not like that. The waking state is the only state available.

At this moment, you are sitting here awake, or perhaps you are half-awake and half-asleep or you may be dreaming, thinking about something else. However much you are awake now, is this life? Is life not more than this? At night, you will leave and sleep.

Life is present even there. When you are dreaming, it may be a different life.

In this way, life has different compartments, but there is no contact between compartments. There are no windows, doors or any other connections. Somehow, you still move from one compartment to the other, though you cannot see from one to another or experience the others.

Earlier, we have come across a *sutra* that says, "*tritaya bhoktā vīreśah*". The same thing is said here more simply. "*Jāgrad dvitīyakarah*" – All the situations that take place in the waking state are not so significant. They come and go. Whatever comes also goes; we cannot keep anything with us. The mind should be this dispassionate. The mind will be dispassionate when *sahaja vidyājayah* happens.

We'll look at an example. If someone were to ask you what you had for lunch last Thursday, would you remember? You may not remember, but you remember the feasts at the marriage reception, the death ceremony or some special holiday and what sweets and dishes you ate there. But for ordinary days, we do not keep much in our memory.

Similarly, all the ordinary events that happen in our lives – some good words, some words of abuse, some good times, some bad times, some anger, some hatred, some competition, some love, some praise – we do not carry these around. We do not need to give much importance to them because they are second hand. The waking state should become second hand. Only then can we return to "*Svātmānanda prakāśa vapuse, atha shivasūtra*". Until then, our mind stays small. We need to understand the waking state as our second hand.

When the mind gets upset over something or someone, and if we feel hatred, aversion and jealousy toward them, this *sutra* is enough: "*Jāgrad dvitīyakarah*" Realise that all these are just happenings in the waking state. We do not fear a tiger that we saw in a dream. If we are afraid, it is foolishness. A tiger seen in a dream cannot be killed with a real gun. Can the jackfruit in a dream be cut with a real knife?

See how beautifully this *sutra* has been woven in. Earlier it was said, "*moha jayāt.*" But if someone says, "I cannot get over attachment. How to get over it?" then it says, "*Jāgrad dvitīyakarah*".

In the waking state, you cry, "My son, my house, my job." This happens not in dreams, but only while you are awake. This is the second hand. Go beyond to the fourth state, to pure consciousness. There you will understand that you have done this many times-you have had many children like this and many families. You have been attracted by many people. You have cried, "I cannot go on living without them." Yet they have passed away, and you will also pass away one day! Now they may have been born somewhere in Africa, and you are in India. You have risen out of many such attachments after getting entangled. Understand that this is the waking state. This will become clear when you reach the fourth state.

"*Jāgrad dvitīyakarah*" – life is a drama. Whatever happens in this waking state is a type of second hand knowledge. It is like a pre-recorded audio cassette. It has already been recorded and you are listening to it for the second time. Or it is like a film, which has been shot somewhere, and when we play it, scenes reappear. Similarly, whatever happens to us in the waking state is just a show or a replay. All of it has already happened in a subtle way. What we see now is just a reflection of life. That is why it is called "second hand."

First, events take place on the subtle level and later they manifest on the gross level. This is not a theory of destiny, but it is the relationship and the distinction between the subtle and gross planes. Everyone has a subtle radiance around them, which can now be seen with Kirlian photography. An ulcer, which will appear in the stomach after six months, is present now in a subtle form, and can be detected now. Diseases that manifest in your body are present in subtle form six months before they appear in the physical body. A manifested disease is "*dvitīyakarah*", second hand. What comes in the waking state comes for the second time. It is a shadow. Only when something exists does it have a shadow. Ignorance is to take the shadow to be real. The *sutra "Jāgrad dvitīyakarah*" is here to make you aware that it is just a shadow. That is why it is important in *yoga*.

"*Heyam dukkhamanāgatah*" – misery has not yet come. We prevent diseases by taking vaccinations before diseases come. This is what intelligent people do. The unintelligent treat a disease only after it is a problem. By chanting and meditation, the problem that has appeared only in a subtle form will disappear. It will be set right. You may have noticed that when you come for *satsang*, you feel some change inside, even if you came with a head full of worries. Once you enter the environment of *satsang*, gaps in your subtle layer get filled up, and the mind becomes happy.

LIFE IS A PLAY

The next *sutra* is very precious:

नर्त्तक आत्मा
Nartaka ātmā
The Self is a dancer.

The same said in reverse, "*Nartaka ātmā*" means the dancer is the soul.

रङ्गोऽन्तरात्मा
Rangontarātmā
The inner Self is the stage.

The Self is like an actor or a dancer in a play. One who dances or acts in a play uses all sorts of gestures to express the *navarasa*, the nine flavors of emotion. Have you noticed how a dancer expresses feeling? He expresses it so completely, with skill and art. If he needs to express anger, he will even use the red of his eyes to express it.

A good dancer has good expressions. He does not require much time to change from one feeling to another, but can switch in a moment. Isn't it? Similarly, in your life, when you get angry, how long does it take you to cool down and return to normal? How much time passes before you laugh again? But a dancer does not need any time. From moment to moment, in an instant he changes his feelings and expressions. This is very subtle. Look at this with an open mind.

"*Nartaka ātmā*" – the self is just like a dancer. A good dancer does not replay yesterday's expressions today. Yesterday he expressed yesterday's feelings, and today he expresses new feelings. New feelings emerge in everyone's mind, but what do we do? We mix yesterday's old feelings with today's new feelings. *Payasam*, a sweet drink has been prepared fresh, but old, spoiled beans have been added to it. It would be fine if it were just from yesterday, but you add in what is a year old!

When we studied in Kannada medium school, our *Bhagavad Gītā* teacher also taught English. In those days, children thought that they should take something every day to offer to the teacher. So any sweet prepared in the house was taken to her. How much could this lady who lived alone eat? So she stored all the treats in a box and distributed them after fifteen or twenty days, when an odour had started to come from them. These sweets had been given to her, and she did not feel like throwing them away. And how could she give away the sweets the same day that she received them, since she still had a pile of old sweets to give away, which were lying in the box. So whatever we gave her, the same thing we received back as old stuff.

We laughed about it and made jokes, saying that the teacher gave us antique sweets. The sweets actually came from our house, but when they came back they had an extra smell. She would thrust them in our hands and insist that we eat them. We took them in our hands, stuffed them in our pockets and threw them away after class.

We carry around old feelings and do not observe new feelings and ideas that come today. The feelings that an actor expresses today only have a place today. This is his specialty.

"*Aatmā nartaka, nartaka atmaa*" – this means that when you are established in the Self new feelings and ideas come up and are expressed at each moment. We mistakenly think that one who is established in the Self or is enlightened has to sit still like a doll. This is because we have seen images of Buddha and Mahavir sitting, always with the same expression. Although nobody has actually seen Buddha or Mahavir, still we make their statues and statues of Adi Shankara. We feel that we have to sit like those statues, so we sit with serious, long faces.

We think that smiling is an offence because the scriptures say that the enlightened should have only one feeling or flavour. We have misunderstood this saying. One self expresses itself in various ways. "*aatmaa nartaka*" – the self expresses itself as a play. The actor who is angry in a play is not really angry. Similarly, any feelings that the Self expresses do not affect the Self by even a fraction. The Self remains untouched.

"*nartaka aatmaa*" – this is such a precious *sutra*. The whole world is a drama; the situations that happen in your life are a play.

We cry when we're in love; in anger, our eyes turn red and we bite our lip; we clench our fists either to fight or from misery; in rage, we shout. These are part of our day to day life, all of which are later forgotten.

All will disappear with the passage of time. As time passes, our worries change, and we find new worries. With a little awakening, if you carefully observe, you will see that no desire lasts forever. Then, immediately, dispassion will come. Even if we are attached, as time passes, the attachment fades. We only lose time; that is all.

Once you understand "*nartaka ātmā*", you will drop your expectations of time. This is called "going beyond time," *kālātīta* or *mahākāla*. The essence of the Self or *Shiva* is called *mahākāla*. A thing that does not have expectations of time becomes part of time. It goes beyond time and becomes a part of time. Do not wait around, thinking that your hurts will fade with time. Wake up and see them as a play, and everything will disappear instantly. Do not sit, deciding to engage yourself in spiritual practices for twenty years to eliminate negative impressions. Where did these impressions come from? Look at yourself as a dancer. Some people say that there are so many impressions left from so many lifetimes and ask when they will leave. Do not join them, quietly sitting and saying the same thing.

"*nartaka aatmaa*" – it says to understand that your Self is dancing. Look at it as though you are playing a role. You are acting in a drama, and for the actor to perform in a play he requires a stage.

The dancer is on the stage, but something has happened. The stage is within the dancer, who is bigger than the stage. Without a dancer, there can be no stage. Wherever a dancer performs, that is a stage. So which is more significant, the stage or the dancer? Although from the outside it appears that the stage is bigger and the dancer is smaller, standing in some corner of the stage, the dancer is more important than the stage. Likewise, our body appears small and the world seems big, and the Self so small that it cannot be seen. It seems as though the breath is inside. But *Shiva* does not see it this way, but just the opposite.

"*Rangontarātmā*" – the inner Self, the heart and mind are the stage. The stage is inside the dancer. This is an amazing way of thinking. The dancer is bigger, the stage is inside him, and he has to harmonise the drama within himself. The drama that you will perform and the stage are both inside. You do not have to go out and ask that the stage be made ready. It is inside you. Usually, so many arrangements are needed before you can stage a play – a screen has to be set up, lighting has to be prepared. A stage is ready only when all these are set up. Yet the stage is inside you. The *antarātmā*, the inner Self, is the stage, and what you see outside is a mere reflection.

The emotions in the mind and situations are important. The dancer is not on stage, but the stage is within the dancer. Just look. You see some scenery – the hills in the distance, trees, stars, moon or sun-set. All these are captured as a reflection on the retina, which is inside the eye. If the reflection is on the retina, then is the scenery or the organ that captures the reflection bigger? Is the scenery more important or the eye? The eye is more important because all the sights enter the eye. Although the eye is bigger than the scenery, how do you see it? The eye appears small and the scenery huge. This is called *māyā*.

The body has a form, but the consciousness, which preserves this body as a body, is not visible. In the stories in *Chandamama*, there is a ghost without legs. Really, no ghost exists like the one in those pictures. Can you imagine what it would mean to have a white head, hands and all other limbs except for legs? The legs are not necessary if one exists everywhere. If the Self is omnipresent, then it does not need to travel, and so it has no need for legs. This has just been imagined and drawn by someone, and we call it a ghost.

People see something like this and say, "I saw my soul!" or they think that seeing one's Self means sitting down and waiting for a ghost to appear. This idea has been so misused that the minute we say "Self" people become afraid. We say the soul is that which belongs to a dead person and not to a living person. We are under an illusion. "*Nartaka ātmā rangontarātmā*."

धीवशात्सत्वसिद्धिः
Dhīvaśāt sattvasiddhih
Purity is perfected by understanding through the intellect.

The next sutra says "Dhīvaśāt sattvasiddhih" – through the intellect comes purity and balance. How do you understand all this? I am talking, and you are listening. How do you listen? The sound enters the ears, but if the mind and intellect are elsewhere, can you hear? You hear with the mind, which listens through the ears. The intellect analyses what you have heard, classifies it and stores it away.

If we put our hand in a fire and it gets burnt, then the mind knows not to put the hand in fire again because it burns. A person without intellect sticks his hand in fire again and again and his hand keeps getting burnt. People who suffer from mental illness always repeat their mistakes. Even if something goes wrong, they do not understand why. Why? This is because they have a mind, but lack intellect. We repeat mistakes over and over because we do not have the ability to analyse with the intellect.

It is through purity that the light of knowledge can shine through us. In order to have the light of knowledge, we need a certain level of purity. "*Dhīvaśāt*" – *Shiva* says understand through the intellect. Open your eyes and see what is happening – "*Rangontarātmā*." Everything is in our eyes. Mind perceives through the eyes. It enjoys smell with the nose and taste with the tongue. Suppose you are eating some delicious food, and someone brings you bad news. Then can you really enjoy the taste of the food? Does it still taste good? The same delicious treat that was on your tongue a few minutes ago tastes bitter. Who is experiencing this? What is experiencing this? Why has the experience changed?

"*Dhīvaśāt sattvasiddhih*" – mind judges a person as bad and arrogant just by looking at him because of the intellect. After seeing him, we decide that he is bad, and we even look for something bad in him despite his good actions. At that moment he may not be arrogant, but from having seen him again and again the mind says that he is egotistical.

Our mind and intellect judge people and situations. This is because there is a lack of *sattva*, purity. *Sattva* means the quality of understanding something as it is. "*Dhīvaśāt sattvasiddhih*" –

do not come to a conclusion about anything or anybody in your mind. A murderer and thief became the sage Valmiki in an instant. This transformation did not take much time, just a few seconds for him. That is why Sri *Krishna* has said in the *Gītā*:

Api cetsadurācāro bhajate māmananyabhāk
Sādhureva sa mantavyah samagvyavasito hi saa

"The mind of a person who has been engaged in wrong doing can be transformed in a few moments by thinking of me." In just a few moments, he can be released from all his impressions and find peace of mind; he can be established in the present moment and in the Self. This is because a person only has to wake up for a little while and realise that "I am a dancer." In a play, some people play the role of *Rama*; others play Ravana and others *Hanuman*. It is another person's job to raise the curtain. If everyone plays their part properly, depending on what role they have been assigned, this itself is accomplishment. The *Rāmayana* cannot be performed if everyone wants to play the part of *Rama*.

This happened once- we had gone to Canada, and the Indian community there wanted to celebrate the Republic Day. The children were ready to perform the *Rāmayana*. There were two to three hundred children there, of which 25 to 30 were prepared to go on stage. The son of the director of the play was perfect for the role of *Rama*, so she gave him the role. However, no parent wanted their child to play the role of Ravana, the villain, and so the director was in deep trouble. Everyone said, "Do not give my son the role of Ravana. You can give him some other part." How can the show happen without Ravana? Others objected, "Why are you giving the role of *Hanuman* to my son?" Lots of people were unhappy. At last the director gave the role of Ravana to her own son, who was better suited for the role of *Rama*. She asked me, "What to do now? I had to ask him to play Ravana." So now the boy that played Ravana was small, thin and young, while the boy who was stocky, strong and tall played *Rama*!

When we do not even watch a play with the feeling that it is only a play, how is it possible to see our life as a play? We are so foolish. Unless we achieve *sattva*, we will not have happiness. The more *sattva* increases in our life, the more happiness we will find. If we feel less happy, that means that somewhere *sattva* has decreased or is missing, but when *sattva* grows, happiness also grows. This is all to raise the level of *sattva*.

"*Dhīvashāt*" – keep you intellect under control. Do not judge anyone and do not hold onto to any idea about or attitude towards someone. This world is like water. Everyone's mind is like water. Waves on the water cannot be still. They rise up and again become still. The wave that was there yesterday is not there today and today's wave will not be there tomorrow. Likewise, every moment people's mind, feelings, role and personality are all changing. Understand this truth.

सिद्धः स्वतन्त्रभावः
Siddhah svatantrabhāvah
A sage is free from the sway of feelings.

We will be wise when we are free from the influence of our feelings. Feelings bind us. We have to be free from them. This means understanding that our feelings are only a play. The feelings that are passing through us at every moment leave us that very same day. But we have bound ourselves by making our feelings into chains. We will only be free when we are able to throw off these chains. "*Siddha*" means one that flies free like a bird, without bondage or restrictions and without misery. He is just natural, simple and easy.

"*Siddhah svatantrabhāvah*" – Let us see how many people around us feel free. For how long does this feeling last? We can be happy as soon as we have this feeling. Staying in jail, you cannot be happy. You need to be free. In the name of love, affection and trust, we steal freedom from others and bind them.

We say, "You are my son (or daughter-in-law) so you have to do as I say," or "You are my wife, who I love so dearly, so you must do as I say." These are hooks we use to control others. We call it love, but it is a hook- "Just look how much I love you. How can you treat me like that? How can you do this to me? You should do what I say because I love you so much. I've given my life for you. What else do you want? So you must listen to me." We treat people like slaves. Do not think you are doing people a favour by showing them love and affection. This is an easy way to make them into slaves. It is no big deal making people into slaves by paying money, by shouting at them or by using power. But the clever ones make you a slave by showing love. You become a good slave. Love and trust become a noose, which later chokes you. Why? Through ignorance, we have bound ourselves with our feelings.

"*Siddhah svatantrabhāvah*" – "*Siddhah*" does not mean becoming an emotionless statue. There are also feelings in the state of *Siddhah*. "*Siddhah*" also means one who is ready and complete. What is the sign that our life is ready or complete? It is when our feelings are free and open. As far as the body is concerned, everyone has a body, even an enlightened person. The body works and requires food and sleep. But what about feelings?

In a jail, you find both jailers and prisoners. The jailer is free to come and go at any time, while the prisoner is stuck. So what is the difference between them? Both are sitting in jail, behind bars. The prisoner might ask, "Since both of us are here, what is the difference between us? I get my food, and so do you. I have to work, and you also have to work even more than I do." Once his work finishes, a prisoner can go to sleep, but a jailer still has work to do. He is on 24-hour duty. So what is the difference between guards and prisoners in a jail? Guards have a feeling of independence. They can go out, and nobody can stop them, whereas a prisoner is held captive.

If you understand you feelings, you will realise that they arise each moment like bubbles forming on the surface of water. When Sri Purandar Das said, "The bubble on the water is not real, oh Hari!" he has looked at life as a bubble and not considered emotions at all. Our feelings and thoughts are just like waves on the surface of the water, and others' feelings and thoughts are also like waves on the water

"*Siddhah svatantrabhāvah*"
Our sense organs are spectators.

Our sense organs are spectators. This is an amazing *sutra*. The whole drama that is happening in the world is witnessed by our senses. And through them you can see inside and outside. Spectators simply enjoy an event. That is all! Sometimes people in the audience sleep through a performance. If you go to South India, the climate is so sunny and hot, people cannot sleep comfortably at home. Once I asked a friend of mine why he went to see the same film every day, and he said, "There is nothing special about it. We only have one theatre, which shows the same film for weeks at a time, and it is air-conditioned. There is cool air blowing, and I can get good sleep, which I can't get at home. What does the movie matter?" Like this, many spectators get good sleep during a movie. Sometimes, a person asked his neighbor to wake him up if something interesting happens. This is how most spectators are.

We do not take time to enjoy the dance or play of the Self. We keep crying, having lost ourselves in some object; or we are just asleep. We do not watch. This is an amazing *sutra*. "*Atmā nartaka, nartaka ātmā*" – this we have not paid attention to. Imagine that you have gone to the market or a place where you can see many people's heads. Sit and watch for some time. What are the different thoughts and feelings passing through their heads? One might be angry, and another happy. Each one is different. When we observe, it looks very strange. Today, when you go home, sit for some time and examine each person's face to find out what is going on in his head.

Even children observe! As soon as they come home, they find out their mother's and father's mood and what is happening between them. They also plan how to achieve what they want. If they want to go on a trip from school, they mention it only if their mother and father are in a good mood. The children discuss among themselves, "Father is angry so we won't ask today. We'll wait to ask tomorrow when he's in a good mood." Then they'll try to make him happy with different tricks. One will show his report card and say, "Look. I got such good marks." The report card may be old, but the father does not have time to check whether it is old or new, and once the father approves the card, then the child asks, "All our classmates are going on a trip. I also want to go. May I? I'll only go if you say so, and I won't go if you say no."

They know lots of subtle tricks. In case the father says no, they will persuade him, saying, "Everyone is going. I'll also go and then I'll come right back home. It's just for one day, isn't it? If I don't go, my friends have decided that they won't go either. I'm not very interested, but for their sake I should go. Even our teacher will be angry with me and say that I don't participate and keep giving the same excuses." They make sure that somehow or the other, their father will let them go.

Observe the dance of the Self. Watch its play. A variety show is happening – you can see this play out in your own home. Watch people's expressions and you can see all of the nine feelings – fear, seriousness, hatred, boredom and so on. Our life, thoughts and feelings are full of these nine flavours. Remember this much – it is enough. The moment you go home, observe: "Oh, this person is in an angry mood. This person is in a happy mood or a serious mood." If your husband brings you flowers or takes you out to a movie or your wife dresses up and applies make up, then he or she is in a romantic mood.

She may have put on make-up to go to a concert of M.S. Subhalakshmi. There, the women in the audience will wear more make-up than the performers on stage, and their saris they will not wear again. The wife might say, "What will others think? They'll say that I have only one sari. Don't you think that's shameful? Maybe it is not for me, but for you it is. It's a disgrace. For all I care, I could go in the same sari that I use in the kitchen. It is only for your reputation that I am going to this trouble." At the concert, who will notice her? Everyone will have their eyes closed, absorbed in the music.

There are nine flavors, or emotions in life. Recognize them. You do not need to do anything except label them. Today father is serious; mother is in a funny humor; brother is terrified; husband is in a romantic mood. Once you label the emotions, then you will start laughing and then you will enter a cheerful mood – "*Rangontarātmā nartaka ātmā.*"

COMPLETE HAPPINESS

बीजावधानम्

Bījāvadhānam

Nurture a seed.

We sow good seeds in a field, and on their own weeds grow with them. What does a farmer do? He removes the weeds. Only when weeds are pulled out will a crop be good. Similarly, we have different types of seeds: seeds of happiness, seeds of pleasure, seeds of sadness, seeds of contentment and seeds of discontentment. "*Bījāvadhānam*" means to nurture the seeds. If you have weeds, remove them. You have seeds of peace, tranquility, pleasantness and love, and if they are not growing well, then water them and ensure that they grow. Do *sadhana* so that this happens – "*Bījāvadhānam.*"

आसनस्थः सुखं हृदे निमज्जति

Āsanasthah sukham hride nimajjati

Sit and be absorbed in the happiness in your heart.

Sit down and soak yourself in the happiness that is experienced by your heart. When we are doing some activity and happiness comes, we are not able to appreciate it. When we are happy and rest, that rest helps us feel the happiness. Otherwise life is spent just desiring happiness. In life, there have been moments of happiness, but we have not appreciated them. Unless you really appreciate happiness, there will not be contentment in life. That is why the *sutra* says sit in a comfortable position where you can have rest and learn to forget yourself.

There is a verse of the poetess saint Akka Mahadevi who was a devotee of Lord *Shiva*, which says: "You do not accept flowers from those whose bodies do not melt. You do not accept offerings of sandal and rice from those whose minds do not melt."

What does "melting of the body" mean? When we are happy, we do not worry about anybody. Suppose you are sitting in a theatre watching a movie, you do not feel pain in your legs, but you feel stiff only after the movie ends, and you stand up. You were sitting there for three hours, but only became aware of the pain after the movie ended. Even someone with arthritis does not experience pain as long as he is engrossed in a movie. One forgets about the body. This is what is meant by "melting of the body." Why do people even have a desire for happiness? It is because they want to be immersed in their own nature. That is why we desire for happiness. Those who are absorbed in their own nature do not desire happiness. They know happiness is their own nature.

"*Āsanasthah sukham hride nimajjati*" – where will those who are seated find happiness? They will find it in their own hearts, in the ocean of their minds. They will bathe in happiness. Happiness appears to come from the outside, but it actually originates from inside. The external object is just a spark. We feel that this or that object makes us happy, but real happiness comes from within, from the heart. When we are in our heart, we experience happiness.

People in Bangalore have a desire to see the Himalayas and Kashmir. When they visit Shimla, they dream of staying there because of the snow-capped mountains. They think it is so beautiful. But the people who stay there permanently want to go to Bombay; they are fed up with the weather in their hometown. We feel so happy going to Srinagar. Go to nearby Ooty, are the people there happy? They feel resigned to their fate and stay there, shivering in the cold. They feel Bangalore is better.

Why is happiness felt during times of transformation? What actually happens during times of change? The mind lets go of one object and leaps to a different object, but has not yet fully grasped onto it. The mind feels happy during this transition period, this time in-between attachments. After a few days, once the mind gets accustomed to the new feeling, it will not find happiness there either. Observe any happiness. Why does it happen? The mind gets absorbed in itself in between two objects; you can experience this when you sit still.

"*Āsanasthah sukham hride nimajjati*" – Discover the happiness that lies in the heart. The mind can be bound by any object or by any thought. This is very important for spiritual knowledge. Take an object that is dear to you and think about it; when you purposefully think this way, worry leaves you. The object leaves you. The mind quiets down, and a wave rises up in the heart. Whenever you experience love or happiness in life, have you observed what happens? A wave, a vibration, courses throughout the body. This experience is very special, but what happens? Instead of observing the sensation, we latch onto the object. When you hold onto an object or thing, you face misery, and the experience disappears. Observe the experience. And with attention, the seed will grow strong. Then, whatever you do, you will do it happily. Whether sitting, walking, smiling, bathing or taking food, it will bring you happiness. No matter what you do, this happiness will never leave. The peak of life is this *Shivatattva*. We sing a song in *satsang* that says, "the one who is filled with happiness"; this happiness comes to us as an experience.

स्वमात्रानिर्माणमापादयति

Svamātrā nirmānanāpādayati

Each one is responsible for raising his own level of consciousness.

Each person is responsible for either becoming happier or sadder. To the extent that one is centered and firmly established in the Self, that much he will find happiness in positive situations. You yourselves have to uplift your consciousness. What do you say? "I leave it up to God. If he wishes, if it is necessary, he will call me." But you do not say this when you go shopping for clothes or for jewelry. For the work that you enjoy doing, you invest your full efforts and work day and night. But if you are called to do some charitable work or *sadhana*, you say, "If God wants, it will happen." You put in your full effort when it comes to worldly matters, attaining righteousness, money and desire. And if it does not suit you, then you will not bother about righteousness either! If there is a desire to do something, then you will spend all your money. For example, to celebrate a wedding people spend all the money they have. But if someone invites you to come meditate for five days, or even for three days, you say, "How can I apply for three days leave? And what will we do with this wasted leave time? If God wishes me to meditate later, maybe after retirement, he will ensure that meditation happens as I am sitting."

You want everything to happen in keeping with our comfort. What do you do for *sadhana* and to reach enlightenment? You leave it to fate, saying that I will go to *satsang* if destiny moves me to. *Māyā* comes to you through fate, which fixes how much amount of praise, success or money you receive.

It is through effort that happiness and pleasure in life increase, but you leave your happiness up to fate, and engage your efforts to gain *māyā*. Are you getting this? You need to change your perception.

"*Svamātrā*" – what is the quality of your life? What level of consciousness have you attained? Who is responsible for this and who creates your life? You create it. Who is responsible for so much dullness in your life? You are the cause. From morning to evening you eat snacks and fried foods, *masala dosa* and *bisi bele bhat*, and lots of it too. Then you say, "If God wills, I will meditate." How can meditation happen? During the day, you will fall asleep! You stuff yourself with varieties of fried, oily foods and then complain that your mind is not steady. How could it be steady?

Keep an eye on your food. If you eat food that is light, it creates a lighter mind. We alone are responsible for our mind, intellect, memory and body. People eat whatever they want and then come, asking, "*Guruji*! Cure my disease!" There should be a limit to your food intake. You have been advised to take less oil or fewer fried foods, still you ignore this advice and eat spicy food. The stomach says enough, but the tongue wants more. You do not set a limit for your stomach and tongue. That is disease!

When there is no disease, then you do not feel like doing exercise or *yoga*. You say, "No, I do not want to do all these. It is up to my fate. Whatever God wants will happen, and I will live out the natural life span allotted to me. Who wants to take the trouble to do so many stretches? If I fall sick, I can take a pill. It's easier than bending the body and doing sun salutations. Nowadays, there are ready-made ways to lose weight." You invest all our efforts in these artificial methods.

What do you do to raise the level of your consciousness, which is naturally available? This needs your attention. You have to see that "*Svamātrā nirmānanāpādayati*".

Consciousness has created this creation out of itself with different qualities. There is only one consciousness, but it has given different amounts of intelligence to an ant, a cockroach or a fly, as is required by each creature. It is not easy to catch a fly. Even monkeys have the right amount of intelligence that they need. Similarly, humans have been given the amount of intelligence they require. Animals use all their intelligence, however much they have, but humans have not used it to its full capacity. Although they have more intelligence, they have not properly utilised it! We are misers not only with money, but also with our brain.

Once there was a brain exhibition, "Brains for Sale," because many people come to this world without brains. There is the possibility that either God forgot to give them a brain or that someone was rushed and did not take enough. Anyway, a big exhibition of brains took place, with various brains on display. There were brains of great scientists like Vishweshwaraya with tags showing their price.

One brain belonged to Manku Timma, a fool in a Kannada novel. A visitor at the exhibition saw its price tag and was shocked: "There seems to be some mistake. The tags must have been switched. This tag should go with Vishweshwaraya's brain." The organiser said, "No, no, everything is in proper order. Vishweshwaraya used his brain very well, and so now it has no value, while Timma did not use his brain at all, so it is very valuable." Most people are misers with their brains and return them without ever having used them.

विद्याऽविनाशे जन्मविनाशः
Vidyaa 'vināshe janma vināshah
When knowledge is permanent, repeated births are destroyed.

"*Vidyaa 'vināshe*" – Ignorance destroys our knowledge, just like weeds eats up a fence. It is not that people do not understand. Everyone has a brain; everyone has discrimination and knows that everyone will die one day, and you too will die. But if somebody dies you say, "Oh, poor thing! He has died." Are you not going to die too? Are you going to live forever? You are also going to die! Why do you forget this? You are not aware of knowledge, and you forget that everything is impermanent.

You keep thinking that someone said this or that. Whatever anybody has said has flown away in the wind. Listen to it with one ear and let it exit through the other. Why should you suffer by storing everything in your head? Attaching such value to what others say and think is ignorance. It destroys knowledge. You waste your time in useless talk and gossip. In this way and through fights and arguments, the little knowledge that you have gets destroyed. Although you listen to everything that is said in *satsang*, all the happiness and enthusiasm you feel there can be driven away by negative talk and gossip. All sorts of fears, doubts and problems appear again in the mind. It does not take effort for bushes and weeds to grow; they shoot up by themselves! You only have to put in effort to grow something useful. Is it not?

Nobody needs to be taught how to worry. It comes by itself. But one has to be taught how to be happy. If knowledge stays permanently, then your repeated births get destroyed, and you will not have to take birth again. We are born due to some ignorance, desire, hatred, fights or worries.

"*Janma vināshah*" – it means that you will be established in unshakable truth, the eternal principle, and the mind will not go through restlessness, discontent and sadness again. *Vidyaa 'vināshe janma vināshah*– life becomes meaningful.

कवर्गादिषु माहेश्वर्याद्याः पशुमातरः

Kavargādishu mahesvaryādhyah pashumātarah

The mantras we use for different purposes have limited strength. Only consciousness has unlimited power.

The various *mantras* and rituals you do have limited strength. Consciousness alone has tremendous power. Your actions and are limited, and the results of those actions are also limited. When you do some good action, its results last for a matter of days, and likewise when some mistake happens, its results remain for a little while. Understand this clearly and rest; rest in the Self. This has been said again and again.

त्रिषु चतुर्थं तैलवदासेच्यम्

Trishu caturtham tailavadāsecyam

The experience of the fourth state of consciousness pervades the other three states.

All the activities you do belongs only to the waking state, but the experience during meditation is not limited to the waking state, it even seeps into the states of dreaming and sleep. If you go to sleep after you meditate, the quality of your sleep will be different. You know about the three states of waking, dreaming and sleep. The peace that is experienced in the fourth state will soak into the other three states too. You do not have to do anything. What does it mean? Even as you speak, part of you is witnessing. While you are asleep, you are aware that you are sleeping. Similarly, many times when you are experiencing a dream, you are aware that you are dreaming. Many of you will have experienced this. Similarly, when you are doing some activity in the waking state, you are aware that you are doing some action and of the thoughts that appear and disappear in your mind.

Watch all the experiences, thoughts and emotions – whether anger, hatred, etc. – as a witness. Then, consciousness crosses over the three states.

मग्नः स्वचितेन प्रविशेत्

Magnah svachittena pravishet

One who is absorbed in his mind comes into his peaceful nature.

You keep entering the minds of other people, wondering what they are thinking about you or what they are saying about you. As soon as you wake up, you start wondering about what you should say to someone: "What will they think about me? What reply should I give him?" 75 percent of the thoughts that appear in your mind are about others.

"*Magnah svachittena pravishet*" – What does it mean to be immersed? You have to get immersed in your own mind, forgetting about what others think or say. When do you get immersed? You become absorbed only when the mind is happy and in a cheerful state. Look at a child. Give him a lollipop and watch how completely absorbed he is in the lollipop. You can ask him, "What are you doing?" or "What is your name?", but the child will not even open his mouth, and even if he does no words come out. You can keep asking him other questions like, "What would you like?" but you will not get a response. The child will not hear your question because he is so absorbed in enjoying the lollipop. Children are fully immersed in whatever activity they do, and that is why they can have happiness in it. They are absorbed in their own mind. Children never worry about what others will say. They are not self-conscious about anything at all. Why? They do not differentiate; they have no sense of the other. They do whatever they like, and their activities have no goal or purpose.

Activities with a purpose or intention are different from those activities without a goal. We call an activity that has no goal behind it, a game, or play. Whatever children do is play. Similarly, what an enlightened person does is also play. Such a person does not have any goal, but they themselves are the goal.

Your goal is not somewhere outside of you. Do not sit looking at the sky, thinking that *Shiva* will descend with a trident and say, "Child, I am happy with you. Tell me what you would like." *Shiva* only appears like this in the movies or on stage. People hold onto these illusions. They look at the sky, and if the sky is bright one day and many meditators are looking at it, they get delusions. This is called *bhrānti darshana*, deluded visions. This is one problem in *yoga*. There will be some truth to it, so you cannot brush it aside as completely false. It is a combination of both true and false. That is why it is called *bhrānti*, meaning a mixture of both. We are surrounded by not one, not two but many delusions in life – it results in confusion.

"*Magnah svachittena pravishet*" – those who are immersed in their own minds, in their self, enter into their peaceful nature. You can find peace only when you enter into your own mind. You find peace only when you are absorbed. In the *Bhagavad Gītā*, *Krishna* says, "*Na cha bhāva yatan shāntirashāntasya kutah sukham*". How can a person who has no feeling find peace? Through feeling, you get absorbed. Anger is a type of feeling. It is possible to get absorbed in anger. Even if a person feels tremendous anger, strength, courage or devotion, if his mind is fully absorbed in the feeling, it will be steady and peaceful.

"*Magnah svachittena pravishet*" – in spite of listening to so much knowledge and doing so many practices, if the mind is still not peaceful and you are not able to enter into your self, it is because you have not been absorbed; you have not sunk – here, whoever wants to float must first sink. Only then can you float. Those who sink will be saved, and those who want to float are swept away. Life flows this way. In whatever work you do, learn to immerse yourself in it. "You do not accept sandal and rice offerings from anyone whose heart and mind do not melt." To be absorbed is to let the heart and mind melt – then you can enter into your own self.

What disturbs your mind? What is your mind? It is part of consciousness, and the energy that comes in the form of consciousness gets propelled out of the mind as thought, and this energy is lost. A person who is absorbed and peaceful does not worry or think too much. You may have observed that the face of a peaceful person is full of consciousness and enthusiasm. If the same person starts worrying, the worry will show. On his face, wrinkles will appear and he will grow pale. Although work might make you tired, a person withers because of worry, not because of work, is it not? So learn to be absorbed.

"*Magnah svachittena pravishet*" – Only when you are absorbed can you enter your mind. Look at it both ways: enter your mind through meditation, and then you will immediately get absorbed. When you are meditating, do not desire to see this or that. You do not need to see anything or to know where you are. This is how to be absorbed in oneself, to forget oneself and let the mind dissolve. Then the result will come naturally. Or immerse yourself in feeling. Even then you will enter your mind. See it both ways.

What an important *sutra*! Suppose you are listening to some divine music; immerse yourself in the music. When you are absorbed, an extraordinary feeling and joy will come. You can practice this now. Sit comfortably, relax and listen to a beautiful song or a *bhajan* full of devotion. Do not open your eyes or move your fingers as though you are playing the drums. As the music ends, your consciousness will be meditative. People who are absorbed in their consciousness will enter their own mind. Repeat this *sutra* and the others one by one.

The next *sutra* is also very beautiful:

प्राणसमाचारे समदर्शनम्
Prānasamāchāre samadarshanam
When you look into the *prāna*, you will be equanimous.

If someone cannot absorb himself in the mind, is extremely upset, and asks what to do now, the answer will be: "*Prānasamāchāre samadarshanam*" – observe the *prāna*, the subtle life-force. That is why it is said to chant, "*Sohum, Sohum.*" Even if someone feels anxious, sad or miserable, after doing *Sudarshan Kriya* for some time, the mind becomes light. After doing *Sudarshan Kriya*, it feels like the mind has arrived home from a far-away place and fund a new life. Thousands of people have experienced this. That is why the *sutra* says to raise the *prāna*. Raise the level of *prāna* in your body through *pranayama*. The flow of *prāna* should be steady.

Actually, when you are unhappy you take short breaths in and long breaths out. However, when you feel happy, the inhalation is longer, and you may not even notice when you breathe out. Have you observed this? When you are happy, you smell a flower with a long, deep breath to appreciate the fragrance. Your inhalation is longer while the out-breath is hardly noticeable; it is less. When we feel depressed, the out-breath is longer and more emphasised. What is happening? The flow of *prāna* when you are excited or distressed is not even. Let the *prāna* flow steadily. *Prāna* should flow evenly through the body.

We say "*Panchaprānah*" – *prāna* moves in five ways. Compare a child's breathing to your own breathing. There is a big difference. When a child inhales, the stomach goes inside, and when we breathe it is the opposite. If you feel fear, doubt, or anxiety it can be seen when you breathe. A quiver appears in the breath. The quiver can be felt in the in-coming breath as well as in the out-going breath. If the breath is shaking, how will life be steady? Life will shake, the mind will shake and consciousness will also shake. Life longs for equanimity, happiness and peace. A river cannot rest until it reaches a lake or the sea. It has to flow. If a river stops flowing, it is no longer a river. It becomes a lake. Similarly, to have peace in your consciousness, "*Prānasamāchāre samadarshanam*" – when you observe your *prāna*, you will be equanimous.

मध्येऽवरप्रसवः

Madhyeavaraprasavah

When you are doing these practices, do not worry if obstacles come up. It is natural that they come. You say, "*Guruji*, I meditated and did everything, but I'm the same person I was. I haven't changed." Not only you, but your wife, children and the people you know say, "What is the use of going to *satsang*? You haven't changed a bit. Show us what has changed in you. What is the point of going?" This is the question that the young ask their elders: "What did you learn by meditating? You aren't peaceful. You still get angry. There was some change – you were better for a while, one or two months, then you returned to your normal behaviour." It is not surprising if people say this. This is "*Madhyeavaraprasavah*" – it is possible that in between, at some places, you will come across such problems. It is not necessary, but it is not unusual if you encounter such problems. It is natural. Accept it as part of the process because in time everything will be all right again. Sometimes you will be lazy, and later laziness will disappear. It is not possible to always be lazy. Anybody, no matter how lazy he is, will one day feel like getting out of his bed and doing something. At some point he will be filled with consciousness and life. Similarly, even a man full of consciousness could become lazy one day.

Even *Vishnu* slept, and not for one or two days but for an eternity – eternal rest! We also sleep, and we put God to sleep to and wake Him up for ten days. Go to a temple and you can see them celebrate *shayanotsava*, the festival of sleep. It is like we are saying, "It is a problem if God is always awake. So we pray for him to give us what we want and then go back to sleep!"

Even Venkateshvara of Tirupati cannot open his eyes because of all the sandalwood-powder we have put on him. He only has *vāradahasta*, gift-giving hands. It is as if we have requested, "Please, keep giving, but keep your eyes closed. Do not open them. Do not discriminate when you give." There is a good lesson here. Whatever you give should be free from any strings. Do not differentiate between good and bad people. What would happen if God started discriminating? "Keep giving me your grace and keep being kind, whether or not I have done good. If you do not do good, who will? Do not look at my *karma*," they said, and after a lot of thought, they placed a mark on his forehead. It is not a small mark either, but a very big one. It not only covers his eyes but stretches down to the tip of his nose!

There is some humour in this and also some fun. The mark on Venkateshvara's forehead was not made just like that. It came after lots of thought in the past. We think that God does not like fun. Actually, God loves fun, and that is why there is so much diversity in nature.

Look at nature. Everything undergoes transformation. New desires keep arising. That is nature's secret and its beauty! The Self is changing. Similarly, you should also be transforming. This is the way to progress in our sadhana. That is the reason the poet Akka Mahadevi said, "You do not accept offerings from those who are not transforming." Why do we say "*naivedya,*" offering? When an offering is placed in the mouth, it will not stay in the same form once it is in the stomach. A banana changes the moment it enters the mouth – some chemical reaction takes place, and as it passes through the throat, stomach, small and large intestines, it keeps changing, and by then it has transformed and had an effect on the entire body. When it leaves out the other end, it will have an entirely different form. Any offering that you take in has an effect on the body. This is a truth. Have you ever thought about this? Just as an offering or what is consumed gets transformed, life is being swallowed by time. As time swallows you, if you move ahead with the wish to transform you will arrive at the ultimate happiness. That is why it says, "You do not accept offerings where there is no transformation."

Do you know why nobody eats stones or sand? Stones and sand will not be changed by a chemical reaction or undergo transformation once you eat them. So they cannot be offerings. Similarly, if you are like sand or like a stone, what is the use? It is better to be an offering, like a fruit or a leaf. That is why it is said, "*Patram pushpam phalam toyam yome bhaktyā prayachchhati.*" However your life may be, whether like leaves, water, the harvest, fruits or flowers, however it may be, offer it with devotion. Your life itself is like the fruit, like the harvest. It is not just that you go to the market, buy a banana and offer it to God. You become an offering, and it is only when you are transforming that you are qualified to be offered.

If in your head you carry the past around – thoughts from yesterday, the day before yesterday, or ten years back – then you become like sand; you become absolutely inert. Experience life anew every day. Then life becomes a proper offering. "You do not accept offerings from those who are not transforming."

THE BODY IS A TEMPLE

This *sutra* is for advanced seekers. Who is an advanced seeker? This is for those who have already overcome laziness, who do not get angry or jealous and who feel a certain amount of contentment. Since they are not yet fully content, the flower has not yet fully bloomed, but the bud is ready to blossom. This *sutra* is for this category of seekers. Some people say, "I go to *satsang*, but something is missing. I am not content. There is some lack in my life. I sing *bhajans* and have organised many *satsangs*. I've meditated, taught others meditation and had them sit and practice. Still, I am not satisfied." This *sutra* is for people in this category:

शरीरवृत्तिर्व्रतम्

Sharīravittirvratam

Looking at all the happenings in the body with love and care is an observance.

What has happened to us? We not only abuse others, but we abuse ourselves. When children make noise, the elders shout at them and the women swear. It is sheer chaos what happens in a house! In this situation, people see no other solution except to punish themselves. So they either cry loudly or make others cry.

We have been abusing ourselves in the name of righteousness. We trouble our bodies to a great extent. Although a person is so lean that the wind could blow him over, he fasts for several days – Monday for *Shiva*, Thursday for *Guru*, Friday for *Devi*, Saturday for *Hanuman*, and Tuesday for Ganesha. They may fast for three days in a week. Not only that, but they do not observe the fast in the right way. They do not eat rice, but they eat more than their capacity of everything except rice. Others fast very severely, not taking even a single grain. In this way they punish their body. If you keep punishing your body like this or shocking your system, then how can you create light or brightness – "*Svātmānanda prakāsha vapuse.*"

"*Shiva tulyo jāyate*" – when you look at *sadhus* and saints, you might not find happiness, peace, brightness or innocence on their faces. Why? It is because they are torturing and punishing their bodies.

There are two types of people. The first type think that the body is everything and will spend their whole lives protecting the body. The second type completely neglects his body. They punish and abuse it and even find some pleasure in it. This cannot be enlightenment. Both type of people have bodies that are hungry, thirsty and sleep-deprived. We should provide for these requirements, right?

"*Sharīravrttirvratam*" – we observe *vrata*, observances. What do we mean by *vrata*? Anything we do with love and affection is called *vrata*, but anything done out of force, thinking, "Oh, I have to do it," is not a *vrata*. Whenever the mind is filled with joy, it is *vrata*. Suppose you are extremely happy. That day you will not feel like taking food. People who are about to host a marriage ceremony for a loved one in their house cannot eat properly, but will be content to take care of the guests. The elderly women of the house will go on feeding everybody without worrying about themselves. They will take only very little to eat, is it not? *Vrata* is that which is undertaken when the mind is filled with joy and kindness.

"*Sharīravrttirvratam*" – the activities of the body are to be treated with respect and kindness; that is *vrata*. Do you understand? The Divine dwelling in the body is saying that he needs food; let us eat food with this feeling because the body is dear to us.

The body is only a body. It cannot be said to be "me" just because it is so near. At the same time, you cannot say the body is not "me" because it is separate. Because this body is near, you can experience the happiness, pleasures and pains of the body more.

As a person becomes more sensitive, he feels more pain when others have a problem. Suppose you are travelling somewhere by bus, cycle or car and you see an accident. You feel as though it happened to you. If someone has broken his leg, you say, "Oh God!" or even if someone cuts his finger, you feel for him. As a person becomes more sensitive, he will feel others' pain and pleasure as his own. Likewise, one feels, "Whatever is happening in the body does not belong to me, and because the happenings in the body are not mine, I have no right to punish it." So, do not punish the body. This is what the *sutra* says, "*Sharīravrttirvratam.*"

कथा जपः

Kathā japah

Each word is spoken with love, like a prayer.

"*Japa*" means that which is born in the mind and makes the mind pleasant. "*Ja*" means to be born and "*pa*" means to care for. That which is born in the mind, sustains our life and leads to an increase in spirituality is *japa*. If each and every word that we speak elevates us, then each word has become *japa*. Do you understand? Let there not be unnecessary, negative thoughts in your mind. For this, do *japa*. When you do *japa*, then you rise higher, and consciousness flows through your body.

A word that when repeated over and over again raises consciousness in the mind and body is called *japa*. You may have seen that these days in colleges if someone loves someone, that person's name is written everywhere, all over the walls and also in stones in the park. Similarly, you can go to any hostel or dormitory and see the names etched all over the place. I met a married man in Delhi, who had fallen in love with a woman, who worked in his office. What to do? He could not share anything at home since he had a wife and children. He did not know what to do. The same thought kept coming again and again. Her name was *Rama*. So he kept writing her name, "*Rama*," "*Rama*," in a note pad. When he was asked for a signature, he wrote "*Rama*." It became such a problem that he started seeing her face everywhere. Even the cat's face looked like *Rama*, and when he went out on his scooter, he would see her face in the streetlight. He would see her face even in the moon. When he saw her face in the cat, he became afraid and so he came to me, asking, "*Guruji*, what has happened? Have I lost my mind? I think about her 24 hours a day. Even in my sleep, I call, "*Rama*, *Rama*," and my wife is angry, demanding to know whose name I am calling! It has become a *japa*. I do not say "*Om namah shivāya*" or any other *japa*. My mind is filled only with her. When I went to the bank to sign a check, I wrote her name and left. Even if I resist it, the same thought comes to mind. What can I do? What is the problem?" This thought has become a *japa*.

When the mind is in love with something or when it is totally absorbed, that same thought will come again and again without any effort. That is what is known as *japa*. Usually, what happens during *japa*? We may be repeating "Ram, Ram," or "*Shiva*, *Shiva*," but the mind is elsewhere, and there is no connection between the words and our feeling. This cannot be called *japa*. Only when a word arises naturally over and over again with feeling and meaning is it *japa*.

"*Kathā japah*" – Each and every word that we speak arises out of love. This is the sign of a *siddha*. If you look at the *sutras* from another point of view, you can say that each *sutra* describes the qualities of a *siddha*, one whose *sadhana*, or spiritual practices, is complete. They honour all the happenings in the body and do not blame the body. Every word they speak is full of love.

"*Yatītāh yathā chittānāh shabdam arthāto dhāvatte*" – When our consciousness is vibrant and alive, then our words will have value. Somebody may casually tell you, "I love you very much," but it is no use if you say it as though you are acting in a play. In films, actors show lots of love and affection, even though there is not a drop of love or affection between them. It is just an act! Many of our words are like lines from a play – life has become so formal, so ritualistic. There is no depth in people's lives. There is no warmth when people ask, "How are you? Are you fine?" The question is repeated superficially, and the person who said it does not even remember that he asked the question. People ask three or four times as a formality, "Where are you from?" And if the reply is, "I told you five minutes ago," they still go on asking. In large functions and celebrations this happens regularly– it is all formal talk, formal business, and life becomes formal.

"*Kathā japah*" – speech itself is *japa*. That is to say, it is filled with so much life. Sometimes, when you gossip, there is no life in your voice because your spirit is not in it. When you watch the television and hear the news, about some violence, do you feel any life in such news? Even a newsreader does not put his heart and soul into it, but just reads whatever was written. It is more or less dry. All our speech is dry. Usually, we ask, "What did you cook today?" You may get some reply, but you do not even care to listen to it. This kind of talking is useless, is it not?

An enlightened person's life is not like this. He speaks with love. His words are like *japa*. "*Kathā japah*" – each sentence he speaks is full of love and truth. Speak every word with care and with love. Do not talk simply as a courtesy. Treat your words as "*Kathā japah.*"

When those who are established in knowledge speak, even if it is just a few words, it will touch our hearts. Although you speak less, speak well and with dignity. Even when you correct someone, or when you praise them, your speech should be filled with life. Otherwise, your speech is lifeless; it is useless. Rise above such talk. That is why it says, "*japa.*" "*Kathā japah*" – in the past, people would see a *Guru* when life became colourless. He would give them a *mantra*, a sound, and after hearing it, their lives would be filled with enthusiasm. A fountain of love would gush up in a dry life. This was known as *japa*. When you remember the *mantra*, life will no longer be dry; it will be filled with juice.

दानमात्मज्ञानम्
Dānam atmajñānam
The best gift is self-knowledge.

In this world, there must be some give and take. It is a constant. We breathe in and we breathe out. We cannot just stop once we breathe in. We have to breathe out. Similarly, everyone is involved in giving and taking. We give some things to others and we take from others too. Whether in small or big ways, give and take is a continuous process. Yet for how long does the gift last? What is the best gift? The best thing that we can give is *ātmajñāna*, or self-knowledge.

What happens at a wedding ceremony? The host looks at the gift, notes the price and reciprocates accordingly. Someone who brings a gift will get a coconut in return, while someone who comes empty-handed will receive a sweet lime. Even there, there are two gift categories. This is not giving.

In the Vedic culture, no work can happen without gifts. Whether it is a happy or sad occasion, gifts have to be given. When someone dies, we give a gift and we also give a gift when a baby is born. Gift-giving is an essential basis of this culture. Gifts are given at any festival. It is customary to give something to neighbours, older and younger brothers, older and younger sisters, sons, daughters, daughter-in-laws, and son-in-laws and so on. This is a very prosperous custom. There is also a secret behind it.

Do an experiment one day. When your mind is dull or bored, take something and give it to someone. Your mind will change. Have you observed this? Give something, maybe a blanket or a quilt, to someone in need, or if this is not possible, then give a few kind words. Only when you give more, will you be able to receive more, but do not give with the intention of getting more. Then it is not a gift at all. So make a decision to give and give a noble gift.

There is a saying, which is very common here. "If we are happy today, it may be from some good deeds done by our ancestors. Our elders did good deeds, and that is why we are well off today." What does it mean? The benefit of the good work we do, the religious acts we perform and the gifts we give is not limited only to us, but extends to future generations. That is why this saying is so common.

If you just collect different things and give them away for business, you will not be completely contented. Have you thought about why they say that you will gain *punya*, or merit, only if you give? Imagine that someone comes to you with an empty stomach, and you give him something to eat. That person will feel satisfied, and then the spirit in that person will bless you: "Oh! This person has given me food. May he be happy." The positive feelings and relief that arise in his mind will bring satisfaction to your life. Do you understand?

Just like the cool shade of a tree offers comfort and rest for the body, whenever a soul finds freedom, it offers blessings, and that is merit. The merit of giving small things is not great. What is higher is the gift of knowledge. What happens when knowledge is given? A person comes out of his misery and uplifts himself up. The soul, which is suffering everyday in the same condition, will feel free, as though it has been released and found liberation.

A person in jail will feel great joy on getting released. He is like a bird trapped in a cage. The bird will be so happy when it is released from the cage! Similarly, every soul is searching for knowledge. When your life is over, you will face only two questions: How much did you love in your life and how much knowledge did you apply in your life?

How much knowledge have you gained? How much have you learned about your own Self? To how many people have you shown love? This is *sadhana*, and this is what is meant by "*Dānam atmajñānam*" Then, whatever a person does or gives, will give rise to self-knowledge. Seen from another angle, in an enlightened person, you can see self-knowledge in every action and every gift he gives.

विद्याशरीरंमन्त्ररहस्यम्

Vidyā sharīram sattām mantrarahasyam

With a *mantra*, knowledge spreads throughout the body and the consciousness.

What is the use of the *mantra*? It affects three things: the Self, the consciousness and the mind. We call it *mantra snāna*, bathing in *mantras*. How do you feel when you sing *bhajans*? It is as good as taking a bath.

People have slightly misunderstood the idea that a *mantra* should be repeated constantly. They have taken it to mean that they have to chant, "*Rama, Rama*," all day and night. If you do it this way, the mind will become dull because the consciousness will not be awake. While they are chanting, "*Rama, Rama*," the mind is thinking about what work needs to be done, but they end up not remembering to do anything else. This is not what is meant by "constant." We have misunderstood it. "Keep bathing" does not mean to bathe all day or staying in the bathroom for 24 hours. Similarly, if someone tells you to brush your teeth every day, it does not mean to brush your teeth all day. When we brush our teeth every day, we are brushing them constantly and without interruption, right?

Similarly, if we hear "remember constantly," it means remember every day and let that thought stay in your mind. This is the use of a *mantra*. Everything is born from *mantra*. "*Shabda mūla*" – the origin, or root, of creation is sound. The whole world has been created from sound. The world in your mind is created from sound, is it not? That is why we have to quiet the mind with the help of sound. When you sit and sing *bhajans* at least once a week that is bathing in *mantras*. If you go to *satsang* every day, that is even better. Join together with three or four people and do it every day. If you do it alone, then you lack the strength of the group. The energy of the group can uplift everyone, whether people are at a lower or higher level.

Consider how a necklace is made with beads. A thread can pass through the beads only if there is empty space inside. If it is full, it is filled with ignorance. Being empty is knowledge. Similarly, when the mind is empty, pure consciousness enters into it. This is why *Krishna* says in the *Bhagavad Gītā*, "You are all the pearls. I am only the thread." All planets and their satellites are pearls. The principles of space and consciousness have entered into everything and made them into a necklace. Similarly, all bodies, all of you, are pearls. The consciousness, which is present in the body, is me. I am like the string. There is no use just having a thread. The thread cannot become a necklace without pearls, and the pearls are useless without the thread, but when the thread and pearls come together, it becomes a necklace. So, value the body, the world, the Self, the mind and the breath.

EMBERS COVERED IN ASH

How does ash form? It is formed by burning charcoal. The same ash formed by the charcoal cinders finish off the charcoal. Similarly, arrogance, jealousy, desire and anger have come from the knowledge in our consciousness. Is it not? You can only desire something that you have knowledge of. If you do not know what *cham cham* is how could you desire it? Is it possible? If in your mind there is a desire to eat *gulab jamun*, then you must know what it is.

Desire arises from knowledge and the same desire destroys knowledge. In a similar way, you get angry because of knowledge. Nobody gets angry without a reason. Does anybody become angry when they are sleeping? Why do you get angry? It is because you did not get something that you wanted. Your desire is unfulfilled. When this happens, you will instantly become angry. Is it true? You become angry because of knowledge. Likewise, where does greed come from? It comes because of knowledge. Why did you get jealous? It happened due to awareness of something. You heard about something and felt that you should have gotten it, but somebody else got it. That is how jealousy begins. Just as the ash that is produced by burning charcoal finish off the charcoal, all these energies are produced by knowledge.

The energies, which arise in this way, are not right or wrong. They are just energies. Without lust, there would be no birth. Without anger, there would not be strength to get work done. Often, people cannot move forward in life without some jealousy. Look at small children. Even they feel jealousy many times! All these are animal energies.

All these energies are in us, and we need to use them in a proper way. Look at a child. It gets jealous. If there are two children, and the mother takes one on her lap, the other child will become jealous as soon as it sees and will come running!

Do you know the story of Vishvamitra? Seeing the quiet radiance of Vashishta, he became jealous. Even though Vishvamitra was a great king, he could not prove himself in front of Vashishta. He was at such a loss that he could not even open his mouth to speak a few words. Vishvamitra's other name was Kaushika. After seeing Vashishta's glow, the king became so jealous that he started to do *tapas*, penance, and after his penance, Vishvamitra gave the world the *gāyatrī mantra*, which is so valuable. After discovering the *mantra* he wanted the title of *Brahmarishi*. Where did this start? Jealousy – simply pride, jealousy and greed.

What was the story of Dhruva? He was greedy. Is it not only out of greed that Dhruva became who he was? Dhruva did penance only out of greed and desire. Is it not? So similarly, all the animal instincts in our life are shadows of knowledge. This needs to be understood. When the source of knowledge is known, then "*Om namah shrī shambhave*" – the consciousness returns to its original state of bliss. It returns to itself. Observe this happening in the mind. That is what the next *sutra* says:

योऽविपस्थो ज्ञाहेतुश्च

Yo vipastho jñā hetushcha

One who is established in the Self understands the origin of knowledge.

Many people have interpreted this *sutra* as they see fit. This *sutra* is misunderstood not just now, but since the 10th century. *Yo vipastho jñā hetushcha* – What is the source of knowledge? Where is the strength in knowledge? Look to the power of consciousness. When we look in that direction, even the ash on the burning charcoal automatically disappears. When ash is removed, knowledge shines. That is what has been said in this *sutra*.

When you get angry, do not blame yourself and say, "I have done so much *sadhana*. I am meditating, but still I get angry." Immediately check where this anger started. Who is angry? Look at it two ways. Ask, "To whom is this anger happening?" or "Who am I?" and you come closer. Or, ask, "Where did this knowledge arise from?" Look to the origin of knowledge, and when you do this, you will find that all knowledge originates in the consciousness, which is inside us. Then the goal of knowledge, the source of knowledge, is understood.

स्वशक्तिप्रचयोऽस्य विश्वम्

Svashaktipracayoasya vishvam

Everything runs through the power of this consciousness.

When we examine our consciousness, we come to know that we create our own worlds. When there is anger in our mind, then it reflects in other people. If you have some feeling in your mind, it will start to bear fruit through others. The power of intention in our mind starts to grow. Grace and control of the mind increase. Our consciousness gains the ability to bless and to curse. This is to say that through our intentions, we create our own world. An enlightened being creates his creation with his intentions.

Svashaktipracayoasya vishvam – there is one more secret in this *sutra*. Right now, at this moment, you are talking, listening, eating, gossiping or worrying – through what power are you doing all these activities? With the energy of consciousness. All the activities in our life happen through the energy of consciousness. Without consciousness in the body, it would just be a corpse. Similarly, what energy is needed for this world to function? The sun's rays. Because of the sun the earth revolves in its orbit, trees and plants grow, and water evaporates and becomes a cloud and then falls as rain. The sun causes all this to happen. The radiance of Being that is in the sun is not different from the radiance of Being in consciousness.

The power, by which water transforms into water vapour, rises up and falls down as rain is the same power by which we see with the eyes and hear with the ears. There is no difference between these two- the energy of life and the energy of the sun. In the *Gītā*, when *Krishna* was asked where he is, he replied, "*Aham vaishvānaro bhūtvā praninām deha māhitih*" – "I exist in everyone's stomach as hunger. I am also the power of digestion." After saying this, he told *Arjuna*, "You think that you are *Arjuna* of the *Pandavas*?

Even *Arjuna* is me. The one who is speaking is me, and the one who is listening is also me." *Svashakti* – The whole word is created through one energy. I am the center point of that energy." This is the essence of *Vedanta* and the essence of the *Shiva Sūtras.* Even if only a part of this *sutra* enters your mind, it will automatically create complete faith, trust and confidence in you. *Krishna* goes on to say, "*Sthiti layauh*" – "I am not only creating all this, but I am also annihilating it. The end of creation also happens through me. I alone am responsible."

How does this come about? Imagine that you come back from the office in the evening and switch on the TV. You are the one who turns it on, right? If you do not turn it on, it will not start automatically. And who watches TV after turning it on? Who switches it off after watching? The TV is switched on by you; you watch it and you alone turn it off when you finish watching. Say you are ready to have a meal, and all the items are placed nicely on a plate or a banana leaf. You will eat to your heart's content and after finishing, you will fold the leaf and throw it away. You do not keep the leaf, saying, "The food was so nicely placed on this leaf." This would be foolishness. Is it not? There is an end to any work that has started. We breathe in, and we also have to breathe out. Can you say, "Let me hold onto all the air that I inhale"? If you say "Let the air that I breathe out stay out," can life continue?

It is the same with creation. "I have created all this from my energy; in the same way I will sustain it and when it is no longer required I will destroy it." This is complete knowledge. You make decoration for a marriage by building an arch and placing banana tree stems. After the ceremony, you remove all the decorations. Is it not? Another example is when you arrange dolls for the festival of *Dassera*. All the preparations are carefully made, elaborately arranging the dolls and making steps with wooden planks, boxes and bricks. There is festivity in each house when the dolls are decorated. A miniature park is created, fountains are turned on, and sweets are distributed to children. Children cry when all this comes to an end – after the tenth day, *Vijaya Dashami*, everything goes back in the box. The elders say, "Everything is over. How long do you want to keep it for?" Then they take down everything.

We created it, kept it for a few days and took it down. Why? This is just like a game. Suppose you draw beautiful *rangoli* (traditional decorative designs made with powder) in front of the house. Do you keep the *rangoli* intact forever? No, it is not. It is so natural for us to draw *rangoli* and afterwards wipe it away. Similarly, an enlightened person creates a world of his own and brings it to an end when it is no longer required.

You wear new clothes and later discard them. Likewise, you make friends with someone, and after some days as the friendship becomes closer, it is possible that it may become sour and end. Is it not? Yet when both people have a deep understanding of the Self then the relationship will not have problems. In any other relationship, which may be so strong that both say, "I am here for you, and you are here for me," a time may come when each says, "I do not know you." Maybe not today, but one day it will happen, for sure. If a friendship is not so deep, then it has less of a chance of going sour. Is it not?

Suppose new neighbours move in next door. You welcome them with home-made treats and talk with them. You share plates and boxes across the wall that separates the two houses. On some days you eat in one house, and sometimes in the other. This will continue for some days, and then a separation will occur, and the story will change. This is only natural. Do you understand?

Do not think that spiritual knowledge is some great thing that exists somewhere outside you. Only when we go deep in knowledge is it possible to keep harmony and unity intact. Until we find the source of knowledge, as long as we are missing spiritual knowledge, or knowledge of the Self, we will only wander along the periphery of life. If this is the case, our friendships will not deepen nor will our problems find a resolution.

तत्प्रवृतावप्यनिराशः संवेनृभावात्

Tat pravrittāvapyanirāshah sanvenribhāvāt

Even though an enlightened person is involved in action, he is beyond action and has attained a higher state.

These are the words of an enlightened one. Sometimes we try to understand others when it is difficult even to understand ourselves! We do not understand our own mind, but we still judge others, what they are feeling and what they are doing! There is nothing more foolish. It is like trying to extract oil from sand. We have not understood this properly. The phrase "extracting oil from sand" means that oil is extracted from the desert, but not from the sand. We have not understood our own mind, yet we try to understand the mind of others. That is what the *sutra* says.

There is not much difference between you and an enlightened person. If you consider his external knowledge, actions and moods, you may not see much difference between your actions and his actions, but it is difficult to understand the enlightened. Why is this? We have made up different measuring rods for the enlightened. We think that it is one who does not sleep or does not smile or cry. *Krishna* describes the special qualities of someone who is established in wisdom: "*Dukkhe vanudvignamanāh sukheau vigataspraham*" An enlightened person is always equanimous. He does not cry, laugh or become distressed. Yet we impose all the qualities that we want to see on the enlightened. Take a look at the Gods and enlightened saints of the past.

Rama became so upset and lost his mind after losing his wife, *Sita*. Do we not consider a person mad when he starts asking questions to leaves and trees? These days, what would you say if you saw someone who lost his scooter keep on asking, "Oh doors, tell me did I leave my scooter in front of you," or "Oh gate, tell me if I left my scooter parked in front of you." and if he continues and asks the street signs, "Have you seen my scooter?" what would you say about him? You would admit him into a mental hospital. *Rama* was in the same state, more or less. As soon as *Sita* was lost, he started crying for her and questioning the trees, birds and other creatures on the way, asking whether they saw her. If anyone had seen *Rama* in that state, they would have wondered what happened to him! But we have faith in *Rama* and do not pay any attention to this story. Instead, we call it a play.

If you look at *Rama*'s actions closely, you can find many flaws, and sometimes you might feel that you are better than *Rama*. You may think, "What is this? He should have advised *Sita* in the first place: 'This golden dear is not real, and I am not going to get it. You can cry if you want to.'" If he were really God, he could have ended the matter by saying so. What were all the problems for? Is it not?

Dasharatha did not intend to send *Rama* to the forest. He felt he had made a mistake and was trapped in his promise to *Kaikeyi.* In certain moods, everyone does this, even to one's wife, and *Dasharatha* had three wives. It was difficult for him when *Kaikeyi* asked him to send *Rama* on an exile to the forest. In his mind, *Dasharatha* wanted *Rama* to refuse. He thought, "As king, I cannot break my promise. I would be held accountable, but *Rama*, as a young boy can say that he will not go, and the whole matter will end there." If something like this had happened, if *Rama* had firmly refused to go into the forest, there would have been no *Rāmāyana*. However, *Rama*, who understood his father's words, but not the feelings behind them, caused his father to face so much difficulty and pain. Then, he went on to create more problems when he set out to catch the golden deer that *Sita* wanted! Is it not?

Was it proper to kill *Vali* while hiding behind a tree? Look at each of *Rama*'s actions. He did not have a kingdom when *Vibhishana* came to him, but was wandering in the forest and himself needed help. Still, he made *Vibishana* sit in the sand and pronounced him king of Lanka before the war even started! This is nothing but politics. And just because a washer-man said something, he sent *Sita*, who was pregnant, back into the forest. Is this protecting the family's honour? What could be lost? It is laughable to be so concerned about caste and family. Seen in this way, you cannot see any virtue in *Rama*, but only flaws.

Similarly, look at *Parashurama.* What good qualities can you see? You cannot find anything. First and foremost, we say, "*Mātri devo bhavah,*" meaning "Mother is the first God." But just because his father told him to behead his mother, he went to do so. A warrior king who was a little insane created some problems, and so *Parashurama* set out with an axe to cut off the head of every king. Is this intelligent? Is it not foolish?

Look at *Krishna*'s life. He did not follow the rules throughout his whole life. His mother and father were tortured before his birth, and when news of his birth became known, they were locked up in jail. Before *Krishna* was even born, all the children who had been born to his parents before him were killed. And after his birth also there was no happiness. He put up with so many difficulties. Nobody else could have lived *Krishna*'s life, putting up with so many miseries. Even as a small boy he had to face the demon *Putana* who tried to kill him, and he also had to fight with his own uncle and kill him.

In *Krishna*'s life, there was no non-violence or truth at all. He told lies from the very beginning. Where can you find the principle of not stealing? *Krishna* stole everything from butter to his wife, *Rukmini*. Nothing was acquired in a proper way. What about *brahmācharya* (celibacy)? He had 16,000 wives. And as for *aparigraha*, this was not one of *Krishna*'s qualities. *Aparigraha* means I do not want anything, and I will not take anything. In the *Gītā* he says, "Offer everything to me." Nobody in the world can be greedier than *Krishna*. He says, "Give me your mind, intellect, and not only what belongs to you, but also your soul and everything else." He tells *Arjuna*, "Be careful. Do not look anywhere else. If you do, I will not look at you again," and "Give whatever you want, but offer everything to me – leaves, flowers, fruits, water – if you cannot find fruit, then offer leaves. And if you do not have leaves, then water. Give me something." Where is *aparigraha?* If you look at it this way, then *Krishna* has not followed any rules, is it not? Yet we worship him as an *avatār*, an incarnation of the Divine. So do not analyse the enlightened by their actions.

There was one person, Gajanan Maharaj, who lived in Maharashtra and smoked *hukka*, cigarettes and so many other things. While he just sat there and smoked, he would tell others, "Do *pranayama* and meditate." People who saw this wondered, "How come this person sits there, smokes and drinks alcohol, yet he gives us advice?" This *sutra* says that even though an enlightened being could do all this, he is above them and has moved to a higher stage. So do not get disturbed by their actions.

Many Jains place *Krishna* in hell, saying that he is not even God! There is not just one *Rāmāyana*. In the Jain version, *Rama* is a non-violent hero, and so he is worshipped as *maryādā purushottam*, the most honourable man. *Ravana* is killed by *Lakshmana*, instead of being killed by *Rama. Rama* was only a witness, who tried to prevent the killing.

On the other hand, there was fighting and war wherever *Krishna* went. Poor *Arjuna* asked *Krishna*, "What is this headache for? I will relax. Let *Dhuryodhana* rule the kingdom. What does it matter if someone else rules?" But *Krishna* forced *Arjuna* to fight. So *Krishna* alone is responsible for the war. *Uddhava* tells *Krishna*, "*Krishna*, it is very difficult to understand you. You appear brave, but why did you escape to *Dwarka*, leaving all your wealth behind in fear of facing your enemies? Sometimes you say that you are God and at other times you say, with all humility, that you are the servant of servants. It is difficult to understand you. In some ways you resemble an ordinary man. You eat and talk. You sit with us and sometimes are confused. You call me for advice, saying, '*Uddhava*, come here. Did I do the right thing? What should I do next?' When you ask for suggestions, I wonder how it is possible that you are God. Yet your endless knowledge, your vibration and charm leave us all amazed and at a loss for words. You have completely opposite values in you."

So what did the Jains do? In one place, they put him in hell because he was not non-violent. In another place, they said that *Krishna* will take birth as the world-saviour in the coming age. They could not completely assign him to hell because he had so much spiritual knowledge and so many principles. As both types of qualities were visible in him, what could they say? Do not see an enlightened being through his actions, but feel his presence.

"*Yo buddhe paratatva sa*" – if we keep our communication at the level of the intellect, then it is impossible to have pure knowledge. Pure consciousness is beyond the intellect. So cross the intellect and move ahead.

OFFERING TO SHIVA

Īshvaro gururātmeti
Mūrti bheda vibhāgine
Vyomavat vyāpta dehāya
Dakshināmūrtaye namah

The river of life is not always flowing evenly. Sometimes it crashes like a waterfall and after hitting the rocks, it rises back up. It courses in between boulders and sometimes runs so softly that we hardly feel it move. Until it reaches the sea, the river's currents and movements take different forms. Similarly, it is difficult to say what will happen in life and when. Life is just like a river. As long as it flows, it is *shivamaya*, filled with *Shiva*, and if it stops somewhere, it starts to stagnate.

On certain occasions we float oil lamps on the river's surface or offer flowers to the water. Some people throw in garbage or planks of wood. The water carries anything you throw in it and moves ahead. Our lives should flow in a similar manner. This is the core of the *Shiva Sūtras*.

Now we are coming to the end of the *Shiva Sūtras*. Let us look at the last *sutra*. "See happiness or misery in your life as though it is taking place outside you." This is an advantage of meditation. Suppose your mind is experiencing some pleasure or it is sad, can you look at it as though all this is happening somewhere else or being shown on a screen?

When people in villages watch movies and their favorite actor comes on screen, they laugh when he laughs, and they cry when he cries. When a viewer is engrossed in a scene, then he experiences happiness and sadness, but if you observe with the awareness that I am only watching a movie, the happenings in the movie will not affect your consciousness.

सुखदुखःयोर्वहिर्मनम्

Sukhadukhah yorbahirmananam

Look at happiness and misery as though it is happening outside of you.

Remind yourself again and again that they are happening outside your mind. Even great people experience misery. After having compiled the four *Vedas*, the eighteen *Purānas* and the *Bhagavathah*, the great sage *Vyasa* wept inconsolably when his son left him and went away. There is nobody more knowledgeable than *Vyasa*. If *Vyasa* had not been born, today we would know nothing about *Krishna*, the *Purānas*, or the *Vedas*. This one sage, *Vyasa*, laid the foundation of India's culture and is responsible for the *Mahābharata*, works on the *Vedas* and other books. That is why when people take the stage to speak, it is called *vyāsapītha*.

Even such a sage fell into deep sadness. He called everyone, saying, "Come, take from this knowledge. With this knowledge of *Brahman,* you will find everything, righteousness, wealth, fulfillment of desires and freedom. I am offering knowledge that will give you happiness in this world." Even when he called, "Please come," nobody came. He wept, thinking, "What can I do? Whatever work I have done until now, is it all useless?"

Similarly, when Christ was crucified, he cried, "My God, why have you forsaken me?" But there is a vast difference between that cry and a cry in the mind of an ordinary person. Suppose you are looking at your reflection in a lake's smooth surface, you can see yourself clearly. If you throw a stone, it shatters the reflection. Now if you start crying that your image shattered and thinking, "I am gone," then that crying is out of ignorance.

There is a story about Mullah Nasruddin. He was under the delusion that he was dead. Many people spoke to him, but he kept insisting that he was dead. Everyone got tired of telling him, "No sir, you are alive and talking." He would reply, "No, no. Even corpses can talk." His family took him to see a psychiatrist. He said, "See, I am dead, but nobody believes me. You at least can convince them that I am dead." The psychiatrist tried several arguments with him, saying, "No sir, you are alive. You have walked here, you are sitting and eating." No sooner would he say these things than Mullah would reply, "No, I am dead." The doctor thought for a moment and took out a blade. He made a small cut on Mullah's hand, which immediately started bleeding.

The doctor said, "See, you are bleeding. Do dead bodies bleed? No, but there is blood on your hand, so you are alive. Aren't your arguments wrong?" Mullah said, "Today I realised a great truth." The psychiatrist was happy, thinking, "My God, his disease is cured, he has realised the truth that he is alive." Mullah continued, "Yes, I realised a great truth. Do you know what it is? A dead body also bleeds."

Similarly, when we have foolishness in our heads, no matter how many discourses you hear or whatever you do, it is of no use. Ignorance should be gotten rid of naturally, with an innocent mind. Then we return to the original *sutra*: "*svātmānanda prakāśa vapuse.*" In an ancient scripture, the results that come from studying it are given at the very beginning. "*namah shrī śambhave svātmānanda prakāśa vapuse*" – the body will shine. A bright consciousness inhabits the body. It is initially in the form of desires and habits. Then, these desires transform into love, and love transforms into pure consciousness.

Pure consciousness, pure understanding and pure knowledge start from love. Desires are below the navel. Imagination is between the navel and throat and between the throat and the head, in between the eye brows lies pure consciousness. Only one pure consciousness shines in us. This alone is called *Brahma*, *Vishnu* and *Maheshvara*. *Brahma* is the creator and creates all desires. *Vishnu* is the protector – everything in the world is sustained only by love. *Shiva* offers liberation, brings transformation and gives knowledge. Our lives should reach the highest level, like Mount *Meru*, and we should cultivate the essence of *Shiva*, innocence, auspiciousness. That light should glow within us, and for this to happen we need to keep going deep in meditation.

What does it mean to go into meditation? So many techniques have been given up till this point. There are already many ways. Life is like a game of snakes and ladders. You climb up and fall back down once you run into a snake. Again, you roll the dice and climb higher. If you hold on to these *sutras*, they will help you in any place, at any time whether going up or falling down in the wheel of life.

Earlier, the *sutras* explained how to get rid of worry. You cannot run away from worry. You have to sit down and analyse it. Then, it says, "*jñānādhinaānah mātrakaī*" and "*chittam mantrah*" – "Your very mind is the *mantra*, and the *mantra* is the mind." Then, "*gururupāyam*" – "Guru is the means." Using various *sutras,* a great effort has been made in the *Shiva Sūtras* to guide us on the path. Therefore, they should be read over and over again. We have a tradition of repeating the *Durga Saptashloki* and other verses 11, 21, or 31 times and so on. This is because when we repeat something over and over again, the knowledge it contains is made available to different parts of the mind. What is the mind? It is not one person, but hundreds, maybe thousands of personalities. Just as there are hundreds of people in a community, there are hundreds of cells in your mind. All of them need to be continually educated over and over again. When can we say that all the people in a village have been educated? For this, everyone in the village has to be educated. Is it not? Similarly, to have complete knowledge, we need to educate all the thousands of cells that are in our brain. This takes practice. By repeatedly going into knowledge, you will experience an evolution of consciousness.

If, for one day, you do not practice, then it means those atoms that came to school that day have lost a chance to learn. Only after one year will they regain the chance. There is a shift system even in a day. Different atoms work at different times. That is why the consciousness needs the nutrition of knowledge again and again. What do these atoms ask you to do after gaining all this knowledge?

शिवार्पणमऽस्तु
Shivārpanamastu
Offerings to *Shiva.*

Offer everything; offer knowledge too. Become the embodiment of knowledge. You do not need knowledge; do not look for it somewhere else. "*Jñānāt dhyānam vishishyate*" – sit, meditate and see that you are knowledge.

The last *sutra* says where knowledge resides. Is it in an object? Is it in the eyes? Where is it? It is in our consciousness. The mind is filled with knowledge. Outside knowledge is only to blossom the mind, which is already filled with knowledge. You should have knowledge in meditation. Know, "I am knowledge. I do not need knowledge." The best knowledge is acquired through meditation. That knowledge is pure and flawless, and will make you content. You will be content to the extent that you have knowledge. Contentment and knowledge go hand in hand. You will be discontent to the extent of your ignorance.

"*Shivārpanamastu*" – We need a small thread to fly a kite. With that thread, the kite can fly to any height. Likewise, every *sutra* has the ability to uplift our consciousness. So read the *Shiva Sūtras* again and again. Have you forgotten all the *sutras we* read until now? Do not forget. Make it a habit to read them or listen to them over and over again. When you do so, you develop a capacity to understand their meaning in fresh and deeper ways.

Question: How do we observe the *chakras*?

Gurudev: Observing the *chakras* means that for every emotion in the mind, there is a corresponding sensation in the body. Sit and observe. Meditate and see the body as a pillar of light. This is a type of meditation. Do you know what happens in meditation? You are holding onto some idea and then you let go. When you let go, you feel infinite rest, and in that state of infinite relaxation meditation and *samadhi* become possible.

Say you are worried or have some regrets, and you have the idea that worry and misery are a part of you. Let it be. Accept the feelings and move ahead. Life is not only this; it is vast and infinite. Let this be your attitude: "I have faced sadness, big or small, many times in my life. I can go through this too." How is this possible? Suppose you have a cold. You keep a handkerchief in your bag to wipe your nose. When this handkerchief becomes dirty, you still keep it on your lap or in your bag. You wash it only after reaching home. You do not throw it away just because it is dirty. Similarly, you may find some disturbances or restlessness in the mind, which sometimes happen because of you and sometimes because of the environment. You may be feeling fine, then someone who is upset passes you by and immediately your heart starts beating faster. Have you experienced this? Or sometimes, without any reason, you may suddenly feel upset. The mind has been filled with different thoughts, concepts and attachments.

There are four types of wishes – *putraitava, vittaitavā, lokaitavā* and *jīvaitavā*. "*Putraitavā*" means "my son, mine, my daughter-in-law, and my daughter" and so on; it is over-attachment to one's children. People get so attached to their children that they do not allow them to leave the house. Those who have *putraitavā* suffer the most and also ruin the lives of their children.

There was a famous family in Kerala, who sheltered their son so much and kept him at home that he was unable to do any work. He could not even go to the bank to withdraw money, and if someone came to the house to visit, he was not able to speak to them, though he was 40 years old. Now the son is unhappy, and the family, including his parents, is also unhappy. They have made him a prisoner in the house. He has been raised in prison. He calls his 70 year old father to accompany him on a trip to the bank. This is how he lives. This family is not an exception. This happens in more or less all wealthy families. They protect their children so much that they become useless. Such things can be seen in society.

"*Vittaitavā*" – means only working, from morning to evening throughout one's life to earn money or to secure property. If someone asks what you will finally do with the money, the answer is: "I don't know, but without it, I am uncomfortable." This is "*vittaitavā*," extreme attachment to money. A person who has this will not spend nor will he allow others to spend. He will not buy anything even for his children. If the children ask for toys, he will refuse, saying, "They will break any toys I buy. So why buy them toys?" He may not need toys to play with, but children do. If his wife asks for a sari, he will say, "Why buy a sari unnecessarily? You have plenty. Wear what you have. Once those wear out, then we'll buy more." He will buy neither what he wants nor what others want.

Once, some children were complaining "When we go for a trip with father, he won't stop the car when we say we want to eat something, but only when he wants to stop." All the food had been packed in the car that morning. The father did not stop the car for two hours, and the children did not get anything to eat because he wanted to travel farther before stopping for food. What is the use of having something when it is not available when we need it? You have enough money, but you do not spend it when it is needed. Instead, you hoard it for your grandchildren. What is the use of such wealth?

Once a businessman called his accountant and asked, "How much money do I have? Till what generation will it last? When can I retire peacefully and relax at home. My hectic schedule has given me diabetes, chest pain, stomach aches and pain in my hands, legs and all over." After checking the accounts, his accountant said, "You have enough for the next four generations that they can live on without needing to work. You have amassed so much wealth!" Immediately the businessman said, "Oh my God, it will last only for four generations? What about the fifth generation? Now I cannot rest. I don't have any time to waste. I could be born in the seventh generation. I have to earn enough for at least seven generations." *Vittaitavā* can also lead one downwards.

"Lokaitavā" – this is the feeling that "Everyone should stop when they see me. They should praise and respect me. People should say that I am a good man." Otherwise, these people worry about what

people think about them. When you are constantly interested in outside objects in the world, this attachment, *lokaitavā,* starts.

"Jīvaitavā" – where do you see *jīvaitavā*? You find it in those who have not fully lived their lives. You say, "If I were to have such a disease or if I had lost my legs or my hands, I would have thrown myself in a river." Yet, at many places like fairs or in front of temples, you find people moving using a wooden plank with wheels. They may not have both hands and both legs. They may have only a head and a body, but even in such a condition, they still desire to live.

Some elderly people who have lived eighty or ninety years want to live for another ten years. They have this wish. People who have not really experienced life feel *jīvaitavā,* the desire to live more. When a doctor says, "Everything is over for you. You are in the last stages. Pray to God. I won't be able to do anything more for you," the patient cries, "Somehow, save me! I have to live a few days more." This is *jīvaitavā.*

These four wishes exist in the mind and in the environment and many times they affect us. So how can we guard ourselves from these influences? Always remember that the *shivatattva,* the principle of the Divine, is present in your body. That is why the *sutra* says, "*Shivārpatav astu*" – offerings to *Shiva*. The last *sutra* is a very precious *sutra.* What can you offer? Who will offer it? What is there to offer? Look at this closely.

Shiva's first name is *Pashupati,* lord of the animals. What is "*pashu*"? This body is "*pashu.*" *"Pashu"* is that which moves on its own without influence from the outside. This body is *pashu,* and its master is *Shiva*. This life-force sometimes bakes, sometimes burns and at other times it blazes. When we become aware of the burning of *prāna*, of the life force, then we move from being an animal to being alive. Who is the master of this burning? *Shiva* is the master. Offer it to *Shiva*.

Somanāth – Who is *Somanāth*? What is "*soma*"? "*Soma*" means mind, the principle of the mind. *Somanāth* is the master of the mind. Who is the master of the mind, of all thoughts, good and bad? *Shiva* is the master. Offer the mind to him. What comes after the mind? The intellect. *Gauri*, the Divine Mother, is the intellect. The principle of *Gauri* is the intellect.

Ātmātatva girijāmatih sahacharā prājnāśarīram guhat
Pūjāte vividhopashauga racana nidrā samādhi sthitih

These lines from *shīvamānasapūjā* say that *Gauri* is the intellect. Who is the master of the intellect? *Shiva*. Again, offer your intellect. "*Īshvara*" means "*ātmanātha*", the lord of the self. Offer it to "*Īshvara*." Offer your self. "*Ātmātvah*" means "*Shivoham*" – I am *Shiva*. Whether you say, "*Shivoham*" or "*Shivārpanam*" both mean the same.

When everything has been offered to *Shiva*, we realise "*Shivoham, Shivoham!*"

The Art of Living
&
The International Association for Human Values

Transforming Lives...

The Founder

Gurudev Sri Sri Ravi Shankar

Gurudev Sri Sri Ravi Shankar is a universally revered spiritual and humanitarian leader. His vision of a violence-free, stress-free society through the reawakening of human values has inspired millions to broaden their spheres of responsibility and work towards the betterment of the world. Born in 1956 in southern India, Gurudev was often found deep in meditation as a child. At the age of four, he astonished his teachers by reciting the Bhagwad Gita, an ancient Sanskrit scripture. He has always had the unique gift of presenting the deepest truths in the simplest of words.

Gurudev established The Art of Living, an educational and humanitarian Non-Governmental Organisation that works in special consultative status with the Economic and Social Council (ECOSOC) of the United Nations in 1981. Present in over 156 countries, it formulates and implements lasting solutions to conflicts and issues faced by individuals, communities and nations. In 1997, he founded the International Association for Human Values (IAHV) to foster human values and lead sustainable development projects. Gurudev has reached out to more than 300 million people worldwide through personal interactions, public events, teachings, The Art of Living workshops and humanitarian initiatives. He has brought to the masses ancient practices which were traditionally kept exclusive, and has designed many self development techniques which can easily be integrated into daily life to calm the mind and instill confidence and enthusiasm. One of Gurudev's most unique offerings to the world is the Sudarshan Kriya, a powerful breathing technique that facilitates physical, mental, emotional and social well-being.

Numerous awards have been bestowed upon Gurudev Sri Sri Ravi Shankar which includes Padma Vibhushan (India's second highest civilian award) and the highest civilian awards from Paraguay, Mongolia and Colombia. Gurudev has addressed several international forums, including the United Nations Millennium World Peace Summit (2000), World Economic Forum (2001, 2003), World Summit On Ethics In Sports at FIFA Headquarters, Zurich (2014, 2016), UNESCO (2015), Parliaments of France, Britain, Norway (2016) and others.

Gurudev has played a key role in conflict resolution across the world including Colombia, Kashmir, Iraq, Ivory Coast, Naxal inhabited regions of India, and many other places.

Follow Sri Sri on:

Twitter - @srisri

Facebook - www.facebook.com/SriSriRaviShankar

Website - www.srisri.org

YouTube - www.youtube.com/srisri

Instagram - www.instagram.com/srisriravishankar

LinkedIn - www.linkedin.com/in/srisriravishankar

The Art of Living

In Service Around The World

Founded in 1981 by Gurudev Sri Sri Ravi Shankar, The Art of Living is engaged in stress-elimination programs and service initiatives. The organization operates globally in 156 countries with one of the largest volunteer bases in the world and has touched the lives of over 370 million people.

The organisation works in special consultative status with the Economic and Social Council (ECOSOC) of the United Nations, participating in a variety of committees and activities related to health and conflict resolution.

In 1997, Gurudev Sri Sri Ravi Shankar also founded the International Association for Human Values (IAHV) to coordinate sustainable development projects, nurture human values and coordinate conflict resolution in association with The Art of Living. In India, Africa and South America, the two sister organizations' volunteers are spearheading sustainable growth in rural communities, and have already reached out to 40,212 villages.

The Art of Living movement has spread peace and transformation across communities through diverse humanitarian projects.

- Conflict Resolution
- Alleviating pain in War Zones
- Relieving trauma in Post Terror Attacks
- Disaster Relief
- Environment
- Education
- Empowerment of Women
- Prisoner Rehabilitation
- Rural Transformation

The Art of Living Programs

The Art of Living programs are guided by Gurudev Sri Sri Ravi Shankar's philosophy of peace: "Unless we have a stress-free mind and a violence-free society, we cannot achieve world peace." To help individuals get rid of stress and experience inner peace, The Art of Living offers stress-elimination programs which include breathing techniques, meditation and yoga. They cater to every age group - children, youth, adults and every section of society – rural communities, governments, corporate houses, etc. These programs have helped millions around the world to overcome stress, depression and violent tendencies. Emphasizing holistic living and personal self-development, the programs facilitate the complete blossoming of an individual's full potential. The cornerstone of all our workshops is the Sudarshan Kriya, a unique and potent breathing practice.

Introductory Programs:

- **The Happiness Program (Age 18+):**
  The 3-day program equips participants with practical knowledge and techniques to unlock their deepest potential and bring fullness to life.
- **Sahaj Samadhi Meditation (Age 18+):**
  Meditation technique that deeply relaxes the mind and rejuvenates the system.
- **ART Excel (Age 8-13):**
  Introduce your children to spirituality, nurture human values, inculcate self-discipline, and develop their personality to be healthy and well-rounded.
- **YES (Age 14-18):**
  Dynamic and innovative educational program for both high school and college students.
- **Prajñā Yoga (Age 5-18):**
  Helps children tap into the inherent intuitive abilities of the mind.

For more information please visit: www.artofliving.org

International Centres

INDIA

21st km, Kanakapura Road, Udayapura,
Bangalore - 560 082, Karnataka
Telephone: 0091 - 80-67262626 / 27 / 28
Email: info@srisripublications.com

GERMANY

Bad Antogast 1, 77728 Oppenau,
Baden-Württemberg
Telephone: 0049 - 7804-973-90
Email: info@artofliving.de

CANADA

13 Infinity Road, St. Mathieu du Parc,
Quebec G0X 1N0
Telephone: 001 - 819-532-3328
Email: artdevivre@artofliving.org

USA

639 Whispering Hills Rd,
Boone, NC 28607
Telephone: 001 - 828-263-4910
Email: info@artoflivingretreatcenter.org

www.srisriravishankar.org
www.artofliving.org
www.iahv.org